Basketry Round Up #3

Sharon Wilson Fuller, Nantucket Lightship Baby Bassinet, woven, oak spokes, rim, handles and stand, cane, ivory and a cherry base, 31" x 17" x 14", 1990. Wood accoutrements: George Wesolowski. Photo credit and copyright: Katherine I. Chabot.

Edited by Shereen LaPlantz
Bayside, CA 95524

Vivian Aron

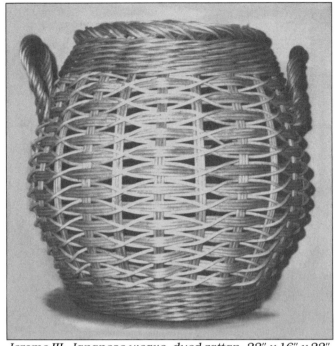

*Jerome III, Japanese weave, dyed rattan, 22" x 16" x 22",
1990. Photo credit: Jerry Evans*

ISBN: 0-942002-08-3
Printed in the United States of American

Opinions and directions given by the by-lined authors belong to those by-lined authors.

All directions included in this publication are based on how the author(s) work in their own personal studio(s). Health, safety and toxic waste removal concerns are not necessarily included in each article -- therefore, following any directions in this publication is at your own risk. The editor and publisher recommend using common sense in all endeavors.

   For further information on health and safety hazards for the artist you may wish to subscribe to: Art Hazards News, Center for Safety in the Arts, 5 Beekman St., rm 1030, New Yor,, NY 10038, (212) 227-6220.

PHOTO CREDIT belongs to each artist unless otherwise noted.

Table of Contents

Diane Dixon

I consider myself a craftsperson first and an artist second, which may be what keeps me working in traditional techniques and materials. Growing up in rural Mississippi I was exposed to several types of traditional basketry including white oak, honeysuckle and cane baskets made by the Choctaw tribe. My first years in basketry were spent weaving Appalachian styles and incorporating other traditional techniques.

Heart Wall Pocket, twill, hand split river cane and aniline dyes, 10" x 8" x 8", 1992. Width of cane is 3/32".

Double Weave, plaiting, hand split river cane and aniline dyes, 3" x 3" x 4", 1992. Width of cane is 1/16".

Double Weave, plaiting, hand split river cane and aniline dyes, 4" x 4" x 2.5", 1992. Width of cane is 1/16".

I have always had a deep admiration for the Choctaw weavers who produced the complicated baskets from swamp cane. As I learned more about basketry, my respect for Choctaw basketry grew. Then fate smiled. During 1985 and '86 I apprenticed with two Choctaw weavers. Since I considered myself an experienced, professional basket weaver, I expected to be making swamp cane baskets by the end of the first week. I did not realize that it would take months just to learn to split the cane. Even then I was clumsy. My splits were short and uneven. And it sometimes took me hours to work through a few pieces of cane.

During the first few months working with the Choctaw sisters I was often frustrated with my lack of progress. Communication at first was difficult. Finally we settled into their traditional method of teaching. When I realized this was how they had been taught, my frustration turned into determination. There were no verbal instructions. I would watch patiently, then try to mimic what I had seen. I have since come to realize that *how* I learned was just as important as *what* I learned. And I learned much more than just basketry techniques, I gained a respect for a culture that has often been overlooked in history. This lead to my ongoing research of the basketry, history and culture of the southeastern tribes.

During my time with the Choctaw weavers, I was taught to harvest, split, and prepare the cane and to weave basic Choctaw style twilled and plaited shapes. This gave me a good foundation. My initial research into southeastern cane basketry taught me the most important element is the cane. To achieve the level of craftsmanship I wanted, I ended up spending four years working on the cane preparation, learning its strengths and weaknesses, plus its limits and possibilities.

The next few years were spent working on different weaves, shapes, styles and finally, designs. I have tried to maintain an integrity with my work; I do not weave designs that are still used within tribes, unless those designs are universal or found in basketry outside of the Southeast. I want my work to be a tribute to cane weavers of past centuries and to not interfere with the few Native American weavers who continue to work with cane.

My respect for the native culture of the Southeast and for swamp cane as a weaving material continues to grow. Continually intrigued by the subject, I hope to persist in my research and the lecturing I began several years ago. The focus of my weaving in the past year has been small scale baskets and miniatures. Flaws are difficult to hide in true miniature baskets. Striving for perfection in miniature helps to sharpen my weaving skills and improve my perception of shape and profile, which follows through to my full scale work.

Cane basketry is both primitive and sophisticated. The primitive qualities come from the cane. Its blemishes, joints and color variations are inherent and unavoidable. The fact that the only tool needed in preparation and weaving is a knife, hints to its primitive origins. In contrast, the complicated mathematical calculations necessary for the elaborately designed shapes are anything but primitive and could be termed sophisticated. Personally, I find the primitive qualities humbling and the sophisticated technical aspects a continuing challenge.

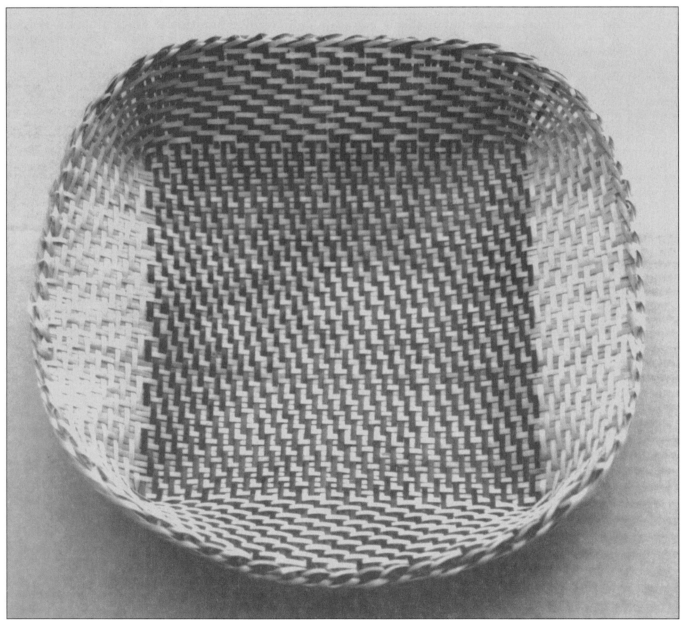

Fanner, twill, hand split river cane and aniline dyes, 10.5" x 10.5" x 2", 1992. Width of cane is 3/32".

Bobbi Hall

Nantucket Cradle, oak base, rims and staves with cane weavers, 32" x 17" x 32", 1990.

Photo credit: Creative Images.

Nantucket Coffee Table, cherry base and stand, cane weavers and spokes, 28" x 18" x 21", 1991.

Sharon Wilson Fuller

Series of Nantucket Lightship Baskets, oval, nesting set, picnic basket and oval tray, oak spokes, rims and handles, cherry bases, cane and ivory, 5" - 20" L, 2" - 14" W, 3" - 12" H, 1992. Photo credit and copyright: Katherine I. Chabot.

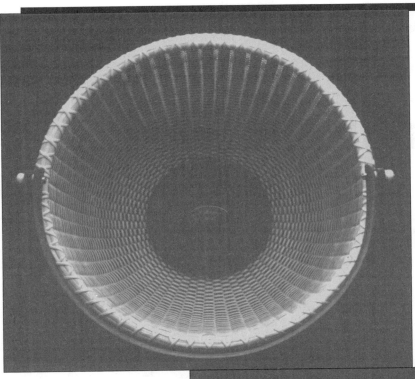

Carol & Dick Lasnier

Nantucket Lightship Basket, mold woven, preshaped, steam bent ribs and handle, walnut and cane, 12" x 12" x 14" OH, 1990. Photo credit: Carol Lasnier.

Darryl & Karen Arawjo

OUR goal as basket artists is to create objects of lasting and enduring beauty. Traditional tools, methods and materials form a strong basis for our work. Using hand split white oak as our primary weaving material, we push the technical limits of refinement and detail. Excellence is craftsmanship is always our first objective. Artistic expression follows naturally.

OUR inspiration comes from a variety of sources and cultures; from respect for tradition and a love for the natural environment, form excellence in all crafts and from the visions within that urge us to create.

Lightning Strikes, white oak, 7" x 12", 1992.

Photo credit: David Coulter

Arawjo Double Wine Carrier, white oak, cane and cherry, 8" x 5" x 15", 1991.

Arawjo Handbag, white oak, cane and cherry, 10" x 4.5" x 7", 1992.

Arawjo Handbag, twill, white oak, cane and walnut, 9" x 5" x 6", 1992.

Susi Nuss

My baskets are all based solidly on 19th century New England tradition. They are a tie to that earlier time. A time when people were more in touch with nature, and baskets were made from indigenous materials to fill the need for functional containers. My interest in basketry grew out of an involvement in my family history. My family has lived in Connecticut for

Market Basket with Curls, mold woven, overlaid curl embellishment with hand carved handle and rims, black ash and shagbark hickory, 9" x 7" x 10", 1991.

Thaddeus Todd II, mold woven with hand carved hickory handle, black ash and shagbark hickory, 10" OH x 9" dia, 1990.

twelve generations. Several of my family's antique baskets were handed down to me. And I have recreated many of them. I often use the names of my ancestors in the titles of my exhibition pieces. In my baskets I try to pay tribute to both the people who made, and the people who used, the simple, beautiful, woodsplint containers of New England's past. I have never felt that the creative process is stifled by remaining within this traditional format. There are so many variations and options within this tradition that it would take me several more lifetimes to exhaust all the possibilities, or be limited in the potential for new discoveries. Maybe I'll be lucky and be granted those additional lifetimes.

One thing that makes much of my work unique is that I process the hand-pounded black ash woodsplint into double satin splints, which means that the splint is subdivided (peeled) twice, revealing the satin-like texture of the interior of the original splint on both sides of the weavers and spokes. The handles and rims are all hand rived, usually of hickory and then hand carved. Each basket is woven over a wooden mold that I have lathe-turned myself. Each piece is made to order, by me alone, and is signed, dated and registered in the collector's name.

Maria Cook's Carrier, mold woven with handcarved handle and rims, black ash and shagbark hickory, 10" OH x 9" dia, 1990.

Feather Basket, mold woven with hand carved handle and rims, black ash and shagbark hickory, 11" OH x 8" dia, 1991.

The Mattapoisett Basket

by Shereen LaPlantz

Gladys Sherman Ellis originated the Mattapoisett basket 20 years ago. The basket style is named Mattapoisett because she lives in Mattapoisett, MA, which is on Buzzard's Bay, not far from Nantucket. (Each of the baskets on these two pages are by Gladys Ellis.)

These baskets started as a means for Ellis to display her scrimshaw. And the scrimshaw continues to be a highlight for each basket. Ellis still does her own scrimshaw and no two pieces are alike, which of course means that each basket is unique.

Each basket also has an elaborate Teneriffe section worked in raffia. The rest of the basket is coiled pine needles. Although Ellis weaves Nantuckets over molds, she coils the Mattapoisett's free form.

Because Ellis teaches this style of basketry — it has become a real *style*, rather than the work of one artist. A number of people in the New England area now make Mattapoisett style baskets.

Author's Note: Last year I got to see these baskets — and hold them. They're incredible! Very sturdy. Fascinating.

Nantucket With A Twist, mold woven, twill, ebony and cane with ebony plaque and catch, 8" x 6" x 5", 1990.

Mattapoisett Handbag, coiled, raffia and pine needles with ivory top and handle, 7" x 5.5" x 5", 1991. Circles and sea gull are whale tooth.

Carole's Basket

This basket was made for Ellis' daughter Carole. It has seven scrimshaw inserts, each portraying something from their time together: the family home, Mattapoisett Town Hall, Center School, Ned's Point Light, Congregational Church, Library and Town Wharf.

With the lid open.

Mattapoisett Handbag, coiled, raffia and pine needles with bone handle and catch, 8" x 6" x 6.5", 1975-78.

Article photo credit: Marcia Jose Garcia.

Lucinda Graf

Let My Heat Reflect, coiling and teneriffe, pine needles, raffia and semi-precious stones, 13" x 9" x 11.5", 1991.

Photo credit:
Taggert Richardson

Only The Heart With Wings Can Fly, coiling and teneriffe, pine needles and raffia, 10" x 12" dia, 1992.

Geodesic Basket

by Billy Malone

The Geodesic Basket was designed and constructed by using three rims placed at 90 degrees to one another. Six God's eyes lash the rims together. Raffia and sisal were used to weave around the God's eyes. Mohair filled the remaining spaces.

Another view

Geo Basket, weaving, raffia, sisal and mohair, 12″ dia, 1991.

A "Look Mom, No Ends" Basket

by Billy Malone

Have you ever thought that just once, you'd like to make a conventional basket with no ends showing? While not completely earth shaking (but we think deliciously deceptive) this basket design shows no ends. Hiding ends between double up-stakes does the trick.

The perennial problem of exposed weaver ends. while annoying, has been accepted as a necessary evil. Basket weaving teaches one to be innovative, at times cunning, and under extreme conditions, some of us resort to outright trickery. And let's be honest now, who among us has not used an occasional drop of glue?

This double-bottomed round basket lends itself to the desired touch of nearly undetectable craftiness. The double pair of up-stakes at the handles and another double pair at 90 degrees to the handles, offer four convenient places for concealing weaver beginnings and endings.

During the initial construction of each of the two spoke portions of the basket, there are two available locations to begin and end weavers. After the two portions are joined, there are of course, four locations.

Wanting to use a over two, under one twill with a step-down, it was necessary to use seven spokes in each of the bottom portions, giving 14 up-stakes total. Together they give 28 which is the magic number (divisible by 3 plus 1).

This method for a "Look Mom, no ends" basket will work using six or eight spokes for each of the two bottom portions if no twill is desired. Just remember to use the double up-stakes and you'll create the magic. When you're asked how you wove a basket with no ends, just tell 'em, "Basket artist's secret."

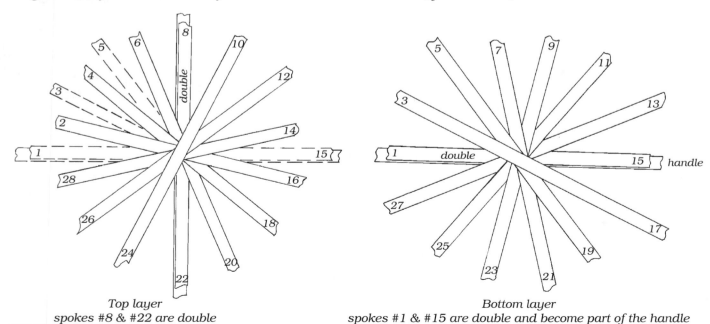

Top layer
spokes #8 & #22 are double

Bottom layer
spokes #1 & #15 are double and become part of the handle

Another view

Look Mom, No Ends, randing and twilling, reed and cane, 9" x 10" dia, 1991.

Laura Kleinmeyer

Lidded Sewing Basket, 4 rod wale, French randing, slewing, skeined handle, roped handle on lide, removeable bottom rim, buff and cultivated willow, 12" x 12" x 22", 1992.

Photo credit: Joanna Schanz

Fancy Laundry Basket, Amana Colony Style, 4 rod wale, French randing, roped handles, flared removeable rim and fancy scallops, peeled willow, 28" x 18" x 18", 1992.

Joanna E. Schanz

Round Shopper, 4 rod wale, French randing and 3 rod wale, peeled and unpeeled cultured willow, 12" x 12" x 6", 1992.

ARC Large Laundry Basket, German willow with removeable bottom rim, peeled and unpeeled cultured willow,

Repairing Antique Willow Work

by Bonnie Gale

PREFACE: This article describes the repair of two antique willow carriage seats plus general considerations involved in the repair of willow work.

Last year, I was contacted by a carriage collector in Maryland to repair two willow carriage seats for an open brougham made by A.T. Damerest of New York in the 1890's. The *brougham* consists of a two-person seat and a smaller groom seat behind the main seat. It had been purchased from the nearby Farmer's Museum in Cooperstown.

The main willow seat

Another view of the main willow seat

The groom seat, front view

The groom seat, rear view

Although I had been sent pictures of the seats ahead of time, I was struck by the great beauty of the willow work. I was impressed by this example of willow use.

The seats were willow woven over an iron frame. They were then bolted to a horizontal board which was in turn bolted in the carriage. The main seat had sustained rat damage while in storage. This had destroyed the willow at the seat bottom where the frame bolted to the horizontal wooden piece. Mainly the damage was located in three positions; the interior left side, the back of the seat and the right side.

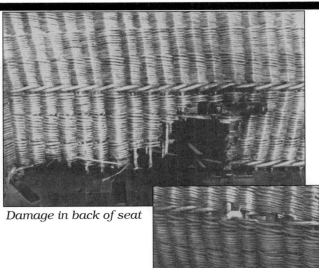
Damage in back of seat

Damage on left of seat

Damage on right of seat

    The repair job was very difficult due to the location of the damage. The seat had been woven from the base up, and, the horizontal board was no long the original. The original base of the seat had holes drilled into it in order to position and hold the stakes (similar to a Swiss willow backpack basket, where large rods are pulled through holes in a wooden base). The board presently supporting the seat had no such holes. As all the gaps in the weaving were located at this junction, I had no place to anchor the replacement stakes — except up next to the original stakes at the top of the holes. Inserting new stakes proved quite difficult (even with a lot of glue).

    Another major consideration in the repair involved the fact that the numerous coats of shellac on the seat held the weaving together, and, under the shellac, the willow was brittle and very powdery. Consequently, it was difficult not to break more of the original willow work while repairing the seat.

    As the original seat had been woven from the base up, the weaver was able to use his (probably not a her!) rapping iron to beat the weaving down very tightly. In making the repair, I could not beat, or pack, the weaving down due to the size and nature of the holes. Hence, the repair could not have the same visual appearance as the original seat. I also chose to repair in a simple randing weave, adding butts to butts and tips to tips, on the inside or *wrong* side of the seat (cushions will be placed here). The original seat weave was English randing. Continuous simple randing allowed a more functional repair. The original weave for the seat's base, after the insertion of the stakes, was a three-rod wale using massive seven or eight foot rods. The missing waling was the most difficult weave to replicate. Soaked and mellowed willow has a lot of flexibility, but willow kinks easily when threaded through tight spaces.

Repairing the seat

Repairing the seat

I wove the seat with white willow and then spent some time experimenting with different stains, trying and match the old patina. I ended up using several coats of orange shellac,

The groom seat had damage to the back (exterior) side of the border. Rather than replace the whole border, I trimmed, glued, stained and shellacked the existing border.

Overall shot of repair

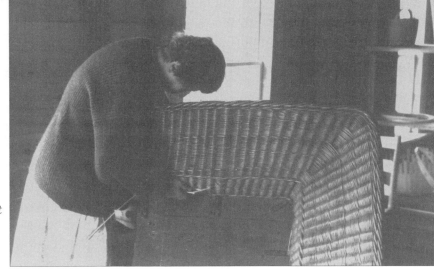

Bonnie Gale working on the seat

Considerations In Repairs

I charged an hourly rate to do these repairs. I feel that it's the only reasonable method for repairing complex willow work. The cost may be prohibitive for customers who expect repairs to be easy and cheap.

If you are considering repairing old willow work, careful thought should be given to the mechanics of the repair before taking on the job. The easiest repair is when a handle is replaced on a willow basket. Most repairs beyond handles can get quite complex.

Due to the brittleness of old willow, there should be consideration of whether a specific piece of old willow work should be repaired at all. Often more of the original willow is broken while making the repair. It is also difficult to make a repair aesthetically match the original weave and patina. The repair can stick out like a sore thumb and sometimes can damage the integrity and value of a valuable antique. Because of the patina factor, clients should always be warned ahead of time that it is difficult to match the color and age of the original item.

The last consideration is that it is often difficult to make the repairs functionally strong. Many repairs can only be cosmetic. This factor will relate if the item is still being used functionally.

All in all, my experience repairing the two willow seats was challenging. However, it was a very special experience to handle willow work made one hundred years ago and feel the continuity over the ages of the use of willow for strong, functional items which support humanity.

Another view

Liz Souter

Lath Basket, lath base, scallomed sides, fitched rattan, hazel wood, rattan and silver bead, 11" x 23" dia, 1992. *Photo credit: K.J.D. Souter*

Wendy G. Jensen

Four Cornered Market Basket, Shaker style lifted base, woven without a mold, rattan, 9" x 13" dia, 1992.

Tall Berry Basket, Shaker style, woven without a mold, rattan, 11" x 8" dia, 1992.

Tall Market/Baguette Basket, woven, rattan, hickory D handle, 20" x 6.5" x 14", 1992.

Double Chain Ash Basket, mold woven, black ash, 4.5" x 8.5" dia, 1992.

Jayne Hare Dane

Stack of Covered Ash Baskets, mold woven, hand pounded black ash, 9" x 12.5" x 16.5", 1992.

Photo credit: Robert Dane

Cass Schorsch

I have always wondered what it is about basketry that engulfs and captures a person. You make your first basket and can't wait to make another. Over the years, I have come to compare the feeling of finishing a basket to "coming home." It's this feeling that generates our minds into thinking about the next basket we want to make.

Return of Spring, 3 rod waling and plaiting, pulled white oak, pulled black ash, white pine bark and white cedar bark, spalted maple beads, 13" x 7" dia, 1992.

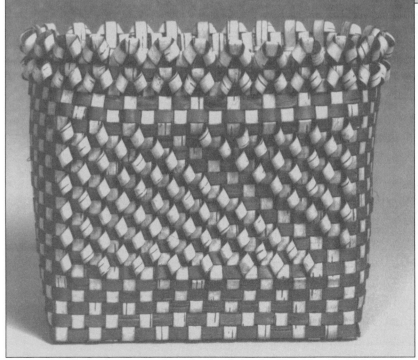

Untitled, plaiting with curls, birch bark, 6" x 3" x 6", 1992.

Article photo credit: Kassandra Fulton.

I have always chosen to weave baskets of tree barks. These materials have allowed me to explore my creative abilities, venture into the woods and develop an understanding with Mother Nature, develop a better appreciation of my senses, and most important — create an everyday challenge. The challenge to send in slides, propose to teach, apply to an art fair, and be able to accept the rejections that come back now and then. This is what life is all about. As a basket artist, I am participating it in, creating it and containing it.

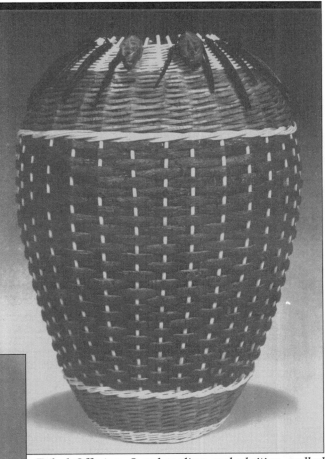

Tribal Offering, 3 rod waling and plaiting, pulled black ash, white pine bark and white cedar bark, 11" x 6" dia, 1991.

Springtime Remembered, 3 rold waling and plaiting, balsam bark, white cedar bark and rattan, 8" x 2.5" x 12", 1992.

Martha Bremer

Untitled, weaving, cloth, reed and cane, 8″ x 10″ dia, 1992.

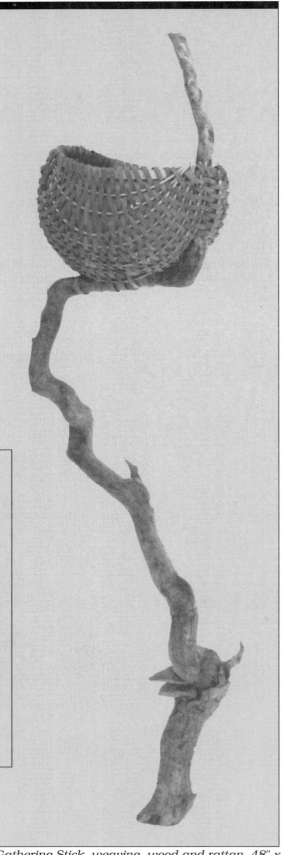

Gathering Stick, weaving, wood and rattan, 48″ x 12″, 1992.

Photo credit: Charles Bremer.

Berry Basket, stitched, folded and laced, birch bark, sweet grass and spruce root, 6" x 6" xc 8", 1992.

Suzanne Nash

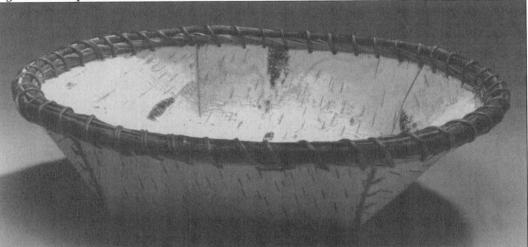

Bowl, stitched, laced and folded, birch bark, sweet grass and spruce root, 14" x 14" x 6", 1991.

Tray, stitched, folded and laced, birch bark and red spruce root, 14" x 8" x 5", 1992.

Basswood

by Ann Lux

Basswood, a material long used by the Native Americans of the Great Lakes Region, can be a valuable natural material for today's basket artists. Processing the basswood and preparing the fibers are often time consuming, but it adds variety to your other gathered materials. Creating your own cordage allows you to control both the diameter and color to fit any design.

Basswood (Tilia americana L.) is a rapidly growing tree native to the Great Lakes Region. It's often referred to as the linden. Found in hardwood forests throughout the Great Lakes states, basswood is easily identified by its leaves which are heart-shaped with uneven lobes and sharp teeth. The wood is used extensively for woodenware and wooden food storage items. It is also highly prized by wood carvers.

It is the bark, however, that is of interest to basket artists. On young twigs the bark is red to green in color which changes to gray as it begins to mature. The bark finally becomes a dark gray, broken by shallow parallel cracks, on older trees. Beneath this gray outer bark lies a fibrous inner bark . This is the layer that's needed for weaving and cordage.

Gathering the Basswood

As with most barks used in basketry, basswood must be harvested in the spring when there is plenty of sap in the trunk. As you wander the spring woods, search for a tree with a good straight trunk, lacking low branches and knotholes. When you find the right tree carefully cut it down. (Note: Always get permission to cut a tree.) Section the trunk into six to eight foot lengths. Larger branches may also be used.

To remove the bark: run the chainsaw down the length, just through the bark layer. Then roll the trunk over and repeat the process on the opposite side. Next, make two *pry poles* from strong branches. Beginning at one end of the cut — work the first pole under the bark and lift. Place

Untitled, triple weave, basswood cordage, 3" x 1.5" dia, 1992.

the second pole to the left of the first pole and lift. Now move the first pole to the left of the second pole. Continue in this manner alternating poles the length of the log until the bark *pops* free. You are now ready to roll the log over and remove the second section. On small trees or branches, the cutting and prying may be done with a strong knife and your hands.

Preparing the Bark

Having removed the bark, it is now necessary to separate the inner bark from the outer bark. Soak the basswood bark for about six weeks in water. You can use a creek, lake, canoe, swimming pool or the bathtub (if your family doesn't object). When the thin layers of inner bark separate easily from the outer bark and each other, the soaking time is up. Remove the bark from the water (it will smell like a dead swamp monster, so be prepared) and separate the thin inner layers. Soak these layers overnight in a large container of bleach water (1 part bleach to 30 parts water) to eliminate the smell. The following day, hang the inner bark on a line to dry. Be sure to separate the individual layers. When dry, gather the bark sheets into bundles and hang them in a cool, dry place. They will store indefinitely if kept dry.

Untitled, twining and triple weave, basswood cordage, 4" x 1" x 6", 1992.

Untitled, twining, basswood cordage, 4" x 1" x 6" (w/oH), 1992.

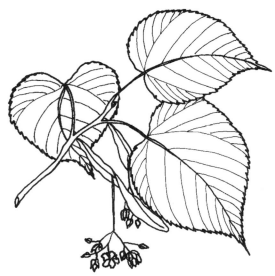

Basswood
illustration by Shereen LaPlantz

Article photo credit: Fred Lux

Making Cordage

Now that the material has been prepared you can begin making cordage. Cordage is a two step twisting process — one twist to the left and one to the right. To begin, take a strip of basswood fiber and split it into widths of one-quarter inch or less. (The narrower the width, the finer the cordage.) Gather four of the narrow strips and tie them in a knot at one end. Use a clamp to fasten the knotted end to a stable object (edge of a table, your work bench, shoe, etc.). Before you begin twisting, wet your fingers and run them down the fiber. The basswood should be only slightly damp. If it is too wet, the cordage will be loose when it dries.

Begin twisting (making cordage) by taking two of the strips in each hand between the thumb and fore-finger. Roll the strands to the right between thumb and fore-finger. Without releasing the basswood, cross your right hand over your left. Without letting go, transfer the twisted fibers from one hand to the

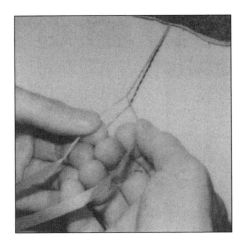

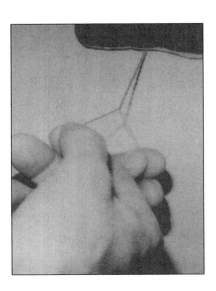

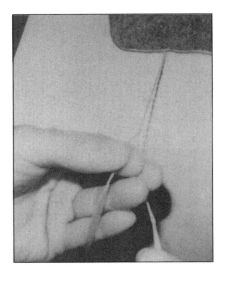

How-to photos by Shereen LaPlantz

other. Repeat the process. Continue rolling to the right between thumb and fore-finger and crossing to the left. As your cordage gets longer, you will need to adjust the material in the clamp.

After a time you will need to add more basswood fiber, either because one side is becoming too thin or because you are approaching the end of a strip. To add material, simply lay the new material on the old, then twist and cross. There will be a small fiber tab sticking out. I do not take time to cut these off until I am ready to use the cordage.

Not only can you control the thickness of the cordage that you make, but you can also determine the length. I usually stop after about three yards, as I seldom need to deal with more than nine feet at any given time in a project.

When you have finished a piece of basswood cordage simply bundle it up neatly and store it. Like the raw fiber, it will store indefinitely if kept dry.

Basswood takes dye well and can be dyed either before or after becoming cord. You can make variegated cordage by dying the basswood fiber and using two different colors when you twist.

Basswood cordage can be used in a variety of ways. Any time that you would use seagrass or some other round material, consider using basswood cordage. Use it when working with other natural materials, such as white pine or cedar. Basswood cordage is extremely strong and can be used for lacing or for handles. As a real challenge, consider making an entire basket or a pouch from your own handmade cordage.

Although it is time consuming to harvest, prepare and produce basswood cordage, there is a great sense of accomplishment when you display a basket of your cordage. I hope that you will enjoy the entire experience and perhaps go on to try cording other materials to enhance you baskets.

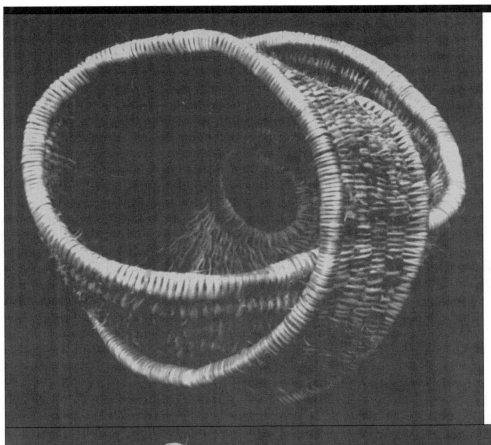

Jennifer Dyer

End view.

Hug Frag-Men-Tation Seven, side view, simple weave, honeysuckle, 13" x 9" x 9", 1992.

Paula Gron

Tripod Pieces, twining with spray and acrylic paints, round reed, embroidery hoops, ash handles, metal rings and tacks, 6" x 6" x 16" and 6" x 6" x 10", 1991-2.

Opposites Attract, twining, round reed with spray and acrylic paints, 7" x 12" x 8", 1990.

Carole Kaeding

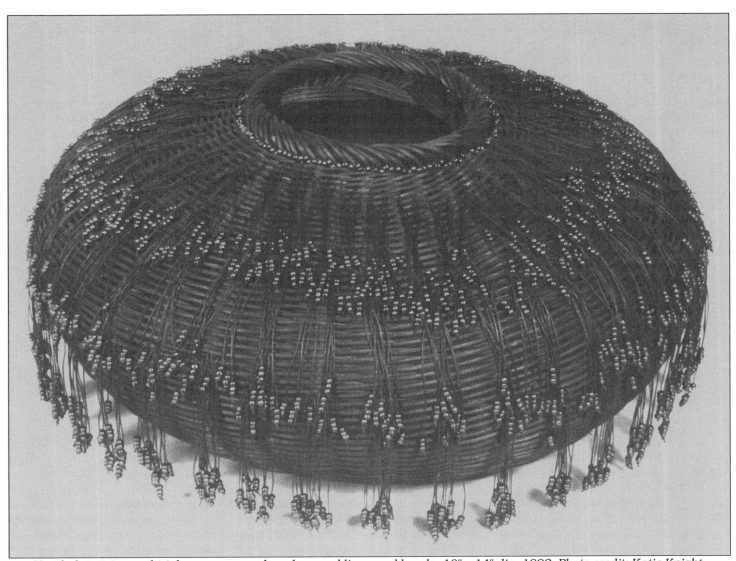

Untitled, twining and triple weave, round reed, waxed linen and beads, 10" x 14" dia, 1992. Photo credit: Katie Knight.

Untitled, random weave, dyed round reed and fish tail palm inflorescences, 15" x 5" x 7", 1992.

Gather Together

by Judy Dominic

Basket artists have historically used available plant materials. Wherever a basket was made, or a technique used, the maker first searched the surroundings for appropriate material. Tremendous amounts of trial and error have gone into determining which plants work the best for the different techniques, sizes, shapes and uses of the baskets. Today's basket artists are fortunate to have access to our predecessors' accumulated knowledge of trees and shoots, leaves and grasses, roots and barks. And vines!

With rattan vine being exported in its natural and its commercially prepared state, most contemporary basket artists have enjoyed using a natural material without having to gather and prepare it. (Although harnessing a tangle of reed in the house at times seems similar to wrestling the vine out of the jungle!) For many years the hardest part of finding basketry materials was the search through suppliers' catalogues to find the best price. This made gathering simple.

This effortless manner of collecting materials offered everyone the opportunity to enjoy the art without as much personal involvement. Reed made learning techniques easy — no sweat in getting the materials and it did whatever you wanted it to do. You could produce a predictable finished product. Commercial preparation made the vine extremely versatile with its many forms (e.g. flat, round, flat-oval, etc.). It also removed us from being intimately involved with our materials, from knowing the idiosyncrasies of the plant and exploring its uniqueness.

Recent changes in reed exportation and concern for the environment make the prospects of personally gathering our own basketry supplies look more inviting. With the price of reed going up, the quality of it going down, and its availability in the future uncertain, it seems like an ideal time to start investigating the local flora. The idea of collecting our own basketry materials fits in with the effort to recycle, reuse and reclaim.

Thoughts of the great outdoors usually conjure up images of peaceful hillsides, magnificent forests and cool breezes. In actuality there are bugs, spider webs in the face, nettles and stickers, soggy footing, steep climbs, tired muscles, and sometimes, blisters and cuts. That's just to get the materials. Then comes the preparation, care and storage. For all the hard work though, there is a wonderful sense of being in tune with your surroundings and materials that is evident in the completed projects.

There are some excellent books that give information on what natural materials to gather plus where, when and how. As with anything else, try things for yourself. A gathering technique that works well for one author may not work for you or your situation.

"But," you say, "I live in a city. How can I collect any materials?" I thought you'd never ask!

Plants need dirt. Go to where there is dirt.

We all know that the *country* has plenty of dirt and growing things. Take a drive out in the surrounding area and see if anything looks usable. Try the county roads; go past the city limits. Find out who owns the property before you collect and be courteous enough to ask their permission. In all likelihood they will welcome your clipping and trimming. If the land is public property, talk with the trustee, commissioner, or county agent in charge. Be honest about your plans to collect — don't *forget* to say you wanted to cut down a tree.

Editor's Note: There are legalities involved, get permission *before* your cut anything!

You don't have access to a car and you get hopelessly lost when away from familiar settings? Don't despair!

Take a walk to your local park and check out what and when they trim. Talk to the person in charge of the grounds and see if they would like some help. You'll even be willing to cart the clippings away! Parks in general do not encourage gathering from their acreage, so be sure you've checked with the authorities

Nested, random weave and knotless netting, grapevine, waxed linen and cocoloba leaf, 8.5" x 8" x 9", 1992.
Article photo credit: Chuck Schauer

Apple Basket, random weave, dyed flat reed, round reed and apple branch, 18" x 5" x 10", 1992.

first. A county park botanist treated our local basketry guild to a program at the park system's nursery. After the program she invited us to rummage in their trimmings — what treasures!

Listen for the sound of tree trimmers as they go through your neighborhood. Keep an eye on the neighbors' yards when its time to trim the leaves and bushes. Scout around after a storm and see what has come down. If any plant material is going to hauled away, you might as well be doing it. Once the word is out about your interest, you'll even have things dropped on your doorstep!

Become friendly with the nearby businesses that have decorative plants out front and offer your services for a periodic trimming. Doris Messick once told of "taking care of" a local fast food restaurant's yucca plants — the free service delighted the manager and was great for Messick also!

Find out about your area garden club (even cities have them). Interest them in a basket class and talk to them about the plants that could be used from their gardens. There's bound to be at least one who would be willing to give you some clippings. A garden club woman from Florida recently saw my date palm work and offered to send me some of her collection of inflorescences!

Stop in to see your local florist. They probably don't carry basket supplies *per se*, but most likely attend trade shows where all sorts of wonderful material can be purchased. At the least they would have supplier catalogues to look through. Offer to order through them and you should have no trouble getting materials.

The neighborhood craft supplier can also be a source for natural materials. KC Siebert tells of buying quantities of grapevine wreaths and taking them apart to have access to the vines for her work.

Nurseries, landscapers, lumber yards, orchards and construction sites are good places to check out possible materials. Cemetery dumps and churches after Palm Sunday may have extra unblessed palm fronds. Be creative in looking for sources.

Other basket artists may be of help too. Ask around at conferences, workshops, or through the magazines or guild newsletters to find out who has access to what. Offer to swap with materials you have, barter or buy outright (do consider the time involved in collecting the materials).

If all else fails, *grow* **your materials.** Ground covers around the house, spring blooming bulbs, trellises of flowering vines, ornamental plants, home-grown grapes and willows — all yield wonderful basket materials. Even indoor plants can supply your needs.

If you are really into "recycle, reuse, and reclaim," don't just stop at plants — *everything* is a potential basketry material. Basket artists already have used clothespins, aluminum cans, plastic tubing and telephone wires. What can you find? If it does what you want it to, use it.

The prospect of collecting your basket materials is not a daunting one, but a delightful one. Understandably, time and labor will be spent. Maybe some physical problems will be encountered. And for many materials you will need to be patient as they cure and dry before you use them. You may not have access to large quantities of any particular plant in a season. You also will want to collect judiciously — leave a healthy portion of a plant and its kind to supply you for the next season.

Using your own processed materials may require you change some of your basketry habits to oblige the personalities, quirks and quantities of the plants. You won't be able to predict (for certain) what the finished product will look like. And you work may not appear as *slick* and *clean* as rattan.

For all the inconvenience and adjustment, the rewards are great. No two baskets will ever look the same. Each piece will reflect the care and consideration you gave the materials. A stronger sense of ownership of your work will develop. A sense of being in tune with your surrounding bit of earth will penetrate your life. You'll be more in touch with the cyclical happenings of your community and its flora (and probably notice its fauna, too). And a sense of satisfaction will be noticeable in having overcome the challenge of nature.

You may not want to stop using rattan reed *cold turkey* — combine it with some of your collected materials and stretch both supplies.

Do consider being your own supplier and create a new basket life for yourself

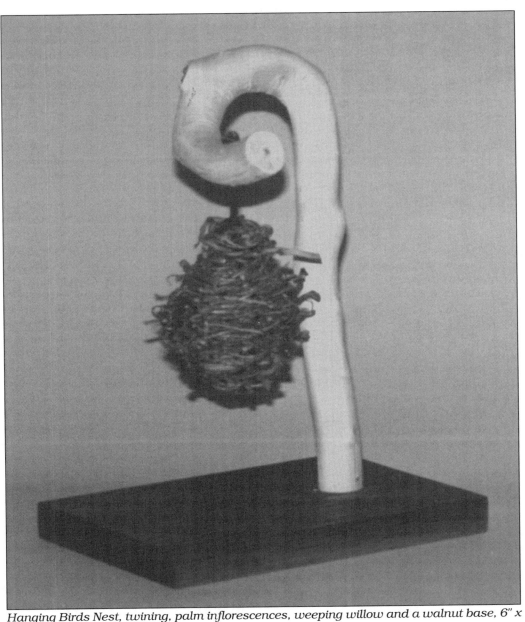

Diane Myers

Hanging Birds Nest, twining, palm inflorescences, weeping willow and a walnut base, 6" x 6" x 12.5", 1992. Photo credit: William E. Myers.

Over the years many people have requested a reprint of the Materials Chart from <u>Plaited Basketry: The Woven Form</u>. Finally -- here it is -- in it's entirety.

MATERIALS CHART

TREES			
NAME	**PART TO USE**	**CONDITION FOR USE**	**WHERE IT'S FOUND**
Eucalyptus (globulus)	Bark	Dry with soaking	Generally used as windbreaks.
	Branches Pods	Green	
Fruit Trees	Branches	Preferably green — can be resoaked, but is difficult.	In orchards
Melaleuca	Bark	Dry without soaking — soaking causes a separation of the layers and deterioration of the material.	Parkways, professional buildings, in gardens, etc.
Willow – many varieties Weeping Willow Purple Ozier Common Ozier Alaskan Blue Willow	Oziers Branches Splints Bark	Dry with soaking.	Near water
Alder	Branches	Green or dry with soaking.	On hillsides, near water.
Paper Birch	Bark Shoots	Dry with soaking.	Forest – near water.
Catalpa	Pods	Dry with soaking.	Gardens – a plant cultivated for the green worms it attracts – they're good fish bait.
Mulberry	Bark	Dry with dampening.	Along fences, in yards.
	Roots	Wash and dry for storage – soak to use.	

Materials chart: copyright Shereen LaPlantz 1982

Please remember the basics about collecting natural materials: get permission to collect and to trespass, leave more than you take so there'll be something to collect next year, and watch out for poisoneous plants.

WHEN TO COLLECT	HOW TO COLLECT	SPECIAL INSTRUCTIONS
Any time – after winter storms or heavy winds – end of summer or fall.	Pick the bark up off of the ground – or gently peel off pieces that are already nearly off the tree. Cut the new growth branches.	Soak in warm water, then cut into strips. Can be used as pieces sewn together. Decorative effects only – so collect and use as fits the basket's needs.
Late fall or early winter – when you're pruning.	Prune – according to the needs of the tree.	Minimal shrinkage when used green. Some barks can be used – experiment.
Late fall and winter	The bark falls off of the tree in large strips or patches – so gather it off the ground.	This is a very fragile bark. It can be used for decorative purposes or the pieces can be sewn together into a form.
Winter – January before the new shoots. River Willow – in the fall – cure one year before using.	Cut the ozier at the base. Cut the branch off at the trunk or next branch. Peel the bark up and down along the tree.	If you run an ozier over a flame several times it will become as pliable as a leather strip. Oziers are generally used round – but can be split using a cleve.
Winter	Cut the branches near another branch or at the trunk.	Run your hand from the tip to the base to remove the leaves.
Summer – to any time	The bark peels off easily or after the shoot is pruned – boil it to remove the bark.	
Fall – when brown and fully grown.	Cut or pull from tree or collect off of the ground.	Split the pod and remove the insides – then split the skin into strips while still damp.
Spring and summer, even early fall.	Fell a young tree – strip off the bark. Dig the roots – find one and follow its length – chop it off at the tree.	This tree is often considered a nuisance and cut out by the city. The roots are bright orange. The inner bark of the root is very strong.

TREES

NAME	PART TO USE	CONDITION FOR USE	WHERE IT'S FOUND
Tree of Heaven (Ailanthus altissma)	Bark	Dry with minimal soaking.	Ditches and roadsides.
Ash – White and Black or Swamp	Wood splints	Green or dry with soaking.	Forest. Black – near water.
Maple – White and Red	Wood splints	Green or dry with soaking.	Forest
Poplar	Wood splints	Green or dry with soaking.	Forest
Oak – White and Basket	Wood splints	Green or dry with soaking.	Forest
Hickory	Wood splints	Green or dry with soaking.	Forest
Basswood	Wood splints	Green or dry with soaking.	Forest
White Pine	Wood splints	Green or dry with soaking.	Forest
Black Elm	Wood splints	Green or dry with soaking.	Forest
Sitka Spruce	Roots – split	Very dry with soaking.	Forest

WHEN TO COLLECT	HOW TO COLLECT	SPECIAL INSTRUCTIONS
Spring, summer, and fall.	Prune the upper branches or fell the tree – then strip the bark.	This tree is also often cut down by the city or considered unimportant by the owner. The bark can attract mold – be careful in storage.
Fall and winter. I have recently heard that felling the tree any time works and that it doesn't need curing in water. Fall and winter Fall and winter	Fell a straight, mature tree. Let it season in water for a month or in the snow until spring. Remove the branches. Make long, straight cuts the length of the tree and the width you wish your splints. Hammer the top of the cuts to pull up and separate the splints (growth rings).	For Poplar – use only the inner bark for the splints.
Late summer or fall Late summer or fall	Fell a straight, young tree with smooth bark. Prepare splints immediately. Split log into quarters or eights – remove heartwood. Stick a knife in between the growth rings and pull apart – continue until the splints are the desired thickness. Split lengthwise to make splints the desired width.	
Spring Spring Spring	Fell a straight, young tree with smooth bark. Make cuts the length of the tree, the width you wish your splints. Pry up a growth ring/splint with a knife and pull free from the tree. You will probably have to keep cutting or freeing the splint fibers from the tree with your knife.	Basswood – the inner bark is strong enough to be cut thin and used as sewing thread.
Spring and early summer	Find a mature tree. Dig to find a root, follow its entire length and chop it off. Don't take all the roots the tree has.	Peel the bark off while still green by steaming or boiling the roots.

TREES

NAME	PART TO USE	CONDITION FOR USE	WHERE IT'S FOUND
Red Cedar	Bark splints	Dry with minimal soaking.	Forest
	Bast	Dry	

GRASSES, RUSHES, SEDGES & FRIENDS

NAME	PART TO USE	CONDITION FOR USE	WHERE IT'S FOUND
Grasses – many varieties including: Wild Oats Brome Hair Grass Squaw Grass Bear Grass Rye Grass Sweet Grass	The grass	Dry with minimal soaking.	Depending on variety – along roadsides, near water, fields, in your yard.
Pampas Grass	The grass – split or whole. The center spine can be used separately.	Dry with minimal soaking.	Along roadways, a a landscaping and windbreak plant.
Mother-in-Law's Tongue (Sanseveria)	Split leaves	Dry with or without soaking.	Roadsides, fields, ornamental gardens.
Papyrus	Stems – split or whole	Dry with or without soaking.	Roadsides or gardens.

WHEN TO COLLECT	HOW TO COLLECT	SPECIAL INSTRUCTIONS
Fall and winter	Fell a straight tree and peel off both the inner and the outer bark – or peel the outer bark by making cuts upward in a living tree.	This is especially good for cordage. Bast is the phloem from the inner part of the tree, a strong, woody fiber.
Any time or fall.	Cut at base as close to the ground as possible. Since these are often weeds, it's tempting to cut the entire plant population – but do leave some for you to collect next year.	Sweet Grass should be collected in August. Rye Grass should be collected in the spring for harsher grass or in the fall after a hard frost for more pliable grass.
Any time	Cut grass at base – be careful – there is a serrated edge.	Remove the serrated edge while still green with your fingernail.
Any time	Cut at base.	Start splitting the leaves with a knife, then continue the splitting with a long, blunt needle. It can be sliced thin and used as a binder. It can also be braided or plied.
Any time or late summer and early fall.	Cut at base.	The tops can be left in place and used as a decorative element.

GRASSES, RUSHES, SEDGES & FRIENDS

NAME	PART TO USE	CONDITION FOR USE	WHERE IT'S FOUND
Cattails	Leaves	Dry with or without soaking. Do **not** oversoak. Do **not** permit to dry while working.	In watery areas — ponds, streams, ditches, etc.
Rush and Bulrush	Leaves	Dry with soaking.	In watery areas — ponds and streams.
Low Bulrush	Stems — split or whole	Dry with or without soaking.	Wet, low parts of fields and river edges.
Tule	Stem	Dry with soaking.	In watery areas — lakes, streams, marshes, etc.
Plantain	Stem — whole or split	Dry with soaking.	Roadsides, fields, parking lots.
Juncas	Reeds	Green or dry with soaking.	In watery areas — lagoons or ditches.
Sotol	Leaf	Dry with minimal soaking.	Fields
Lily Turf (Liriope)	Leaves	Dry with minimal soaking.	A ground cover and border plant — wet areas.

WHEN TO COLLECT	HOW TO COLLECT	SPECIAL INSTRUCTIONS
Late summer and fall — when mature.	Cut leaf at base – pick only the green ones, the dry ones are too brittle.	Thread the leaves together like a very loose grass skirt and hang to dry. 100% shrinkage. If the leaves dry in the shade they'll retain their green color – the sun fades them to a light tan – but this does not affect their performance. Cattails can be plied to make an incredibly strong cord after breaking down the inner fiber and soaking.
Mid-summer	Cut leaf at base.	Cut only every other year.
Fall	Cut the stems off at the base.	
Late summer to early winter	Cut stem at base.	Mash the three-sided stem flat to use – a wringer from an old washing machine works well.
Spring	Cut stem at base.	
Spring and summer for a green. Fall for tan. Winter for grey.	Carefully cut at base – there's a thorn at the tip, so push clump away from you and cut. Remove thorns immediately.	Looks like round reed. It will retain its green color if dried out of the sun.
Any time	Cut at base.	Edges **severely** serrated – be careful – the edge can be split off.
Winter	Cut back old foliage – shaggy in appearance.	

GRASSES, RUSHES, SEDGES & FRIENDS

NAME	PART TO USE	CONDITION FOR USE	WHERE IT'S FOUND
Bull Kelp Sea Grass most Sea Weed	Long runners Leaves	Use immediately.	Beaches
Cane — Swamp and River	Cane stem, whole or split	Dry with soaking.	Watery areas
Bamboo	Stem — whole or split Leaves	Dry with soaking — green if using it whole.	Gardens, vacant lots, arboretums.

VINES & CREEPERS

NAME	PART TO USE	CONDITION FOR USE	WHERE IT'S FOUND
Ivy	Runners	Green or dry with soaking. Some types don't soak well.	Used as a ground cover — try a University.
Grapevine	Runners The bark can be braided into a cord	Green or dry with soaking. Some people feel it is necessary to boil rather than soak.	In a garden, on fences, climbing trees, a winery.
Honeysuckle	Runners	Preferably green — but can dry and resoak.	In a garden, climbing fences.
Wisteria	Runners Bark	Green	In a garden, old arbors, sides of building.
Virginia Creeper	Runners	Green or dry with soaking.	A ground cover, also climbing trees near water.

WHEN TO COLLECT	HOW TO COLLECT	SPECIAL INSTRUCTIONS
Winter	Gather on beach.	Let dry in the sun to cure — but use while it's still pliable. May dampen if stiff but do not soak. Dries in interesting shapes.
Summer	Cut at base — in the water.	
Any time	Cut at base — can just gather after the gardener has thinned the stand.	Bend fresh stems over a flame. It is very difficult to split or saw when dry — and it is readily available in stores. Be careful of splinters.
Early summer	Cut the new growth — about one year's worth.	Strip off the leaves. Can be used peeled or unpeeled.
Fall and early winter for the smooth bark variety. Any time for the shaggy bark variety.	Cut runners on mature plants to the desired length.	Smooth bark variety — strip the leaves and small branches — leave the tendrils. Shaggy bark variety — remove leaves, but not tendrils — coil and boil for four hours, the bark should strip off easily then.
Easiest to find in the fall — but can be collected any time.	Cut the runner and strip the leaves.	To peel — boil for four hours and soak overnight.
Fall — when mature.	Cut the runners the desired length — strip the leaves.	If you're good at cutting — the bark can be cut into splints.
Any time	Cut what you want.	

VINES & CREEPERS

NAME	PART TO USE	CONDITION FOR USE	WHERE IT'S FOUND
Jasmine – many varieties and almost all work	Vine Roots	Preferably green – dry with soaking, but hard to resoak.	In gardens, around front porches, fences, etc.
Periwinkle, Myrtle	Runners	Green or dry with soaking.	Trailing ground cover – on slopes, rough or unused areas.
Morning Glory	Runners	Dry in the shade until barely flexible – then use immediately – for minimal shrinkage.	In a garden, on a fence, trellis, etc.
Giant Smilax	Runners	Dry with soaking.	
Mandevilla	Runners	Green or dry with soaking.	Climbing vine.
Berries – Blackberries Raspberries Boysenberries	Runners (Canes)	Green or dry with soaking.	In your garden, along roadways.

BULBS

NAME	PART TO USE	CONDITION FOR USE	WHERE IT'S FOUND
Daffodils, Day Lilies, Narcissus, Fire-cracker Lily, Iris, etc.	Leaves	Dry with minimal soaking.	In gardens and on hillsides.
Watsonia	Leaves	Dry with soaking.	In your garden.

WHEN TO COLLECT	HOW TO COLLECT	SPECIAL INSTRUCTIONS
Fall and winter — depending on variety.	Cut what you want — strip the leaves.	This doesn't shrink when used green. Leave the bark on.
Winter and spring	Cut what you want.	Keeps its green color.
Late summer and early fall.	Cut at desired length or after flowering — cut back entire plant — it's an annual.	
Any time — but winter is best.	Cut runners at desired length — clip off thorns.	Shrinkage if used green.
Early summer	Cut the new growth — strip off the leaves.	
Late fall and winter — after berries have been harvested.	Cut cane at desired length. Leave enough for next year's berry harvest.	Wearing gloves — strip thorns by running hand from tip to base — the other way strips the leaves.
After flowering or when they are completely dry.	Pull the dry leaves at base or gather the dry leaves off of the ground.	For extra strength — divide and braid or twist into two or three ply.
After flowering.	Pull the leaves at base or gather the dry leaves off of the ground.	Sometimes has decorative tips.

BULBS

NAME	PART TO USE	CONDITION FOR USE	WHERE IT'S FOUND
Gladiolus	Leaves	Dry with minimal soaking.	In your garden.
Lily of the Nile (Agapanthus)	Leaves Split flower stem	Dry with soaking.	Ornamental gardens, shopping centers.
Montbreia Crocosmia	Leaves	Dry with minimal soaking.	In a garden.
Baboon Flower (Babiana)	Leaves – whole or split	Dry with soaking.	In gardens – an accent plant.

PALMS & YUCCAS

NAME	PART TO USE	CONDITION FOR USE	WHERE IT'S FOUND
Palms – many varieties – try all of them	Leaves Bark (coir) Cuffs – whole or split Inflorescens (fruit sticks)	Green. Dry without soaking. Dry with extensive soaking. Dry – some varieties need extensive soaking or boiling.	Along roadways, giant landscaping plant, in gardens.
Palmetto – Saw and Sabal	Fan leaves	Green or dry with soaking.	Edge of water, swampy areas, gardens.
Lauhala	Leaves (Pandanus)	Green or dry with or without soaking.	Tropical plant – in gardens.

WHEN TO COLLECT	HOW TO COLLECT	SPECIAL INSTRUCTIONS
After flowering.	Pull the dry leaves at base or gather dry ones off of the ground.	
After flowering, late summer or early fall.	Cut leaf or stem at base, then dry evenly.	Dry Indoors – extremely fragile.
After flowering, late summer or early fall.	Pull the dry leaves at base or gather dry ones off of the ground.	It has a decorative tip.
Fall and winter are best – but any time works.	Cut leaf at base.	The leaves dry black or charcoal grey.
Any time – after a storm – it's impractical to climb a ladder to collect.	Gather cuffs, leaves, and inflorescens off of the ground or follow a gardener, city maintenance, etc. Bark can be cut off of the tree with a knife. This is **very** dirty work.	A six-foot or eight-foot pruner can cut off fresh material – which is preferred. Cabbage palm stems can be cut green and then cut into splints.
Any time	Cut fan at base – split into strips.	For a more pliable fan – select a tender, young frond from a mature tree – one that is just about to open.
Any time	Pull leaf from stem, collect the older, dry leaves, towards the bottom – leave the top, green leaves.	To prepare for use: Pull the leaf over the edge of a desk or piece of wood several times – topside and under-side. Then roll into a coil, one way then the opposite way – several times. Or purchase in a store.

PALMS & YUCCAS

NAME	PART TO USE	CONDITION FOR USE	WHERE IT'S FOUND
Yucca – many varieties	Leaves – whole or split Flowering stalk, short – like 6"	Dry with extensive soaking.	The desert – also a landscaping plant.
Dracena – many varieties	Leaves	Dry with or without soaking.	Gardens, the desert, and a landscape plant.

MISCELLANEOUS

NAME	PART TO USE	CONDITION FOR USE	WHERE IT'S FOUND
New Zealand Flax	Leaves	Green. Dry leaves require extensive soaking – like three days.	A landscaping plant – usually around government or professional buildings.
Century Plant (Agave)	White inner fibers	As is after processing.	Hillsides, roadsides, a landscaping plant.
Aloe – a succulent in the lily family	Leaves – whole or split	Dry with soaking.	In gardens and along roadways near water.

WHEN TO COLLECT	HOW TO COLLECT	SPECIAL INSTRUCTIONS
Late spring and early summer – some varieties any time.	Pull the leaves from the base. Twist flowering stalk until it comes free.	Dry and cure the leaves by threading them together like a **loose, loose** grass skirt – and hang them up for six or more months. The leaves from the flowering stalk can be peeled open and spread in the sun. Turn them frequently – one day should be sufficient to dry and bleach them.
Any time	Pull off the dry, dead leaves.	*Dracena draco* has apricot tips.
Any time – but best in the fall.	Cut the leaves close to the base or where they bend over.	Expect 50% shrinkage.
Any time	Cut the sword-like leaves at the base. Then pound them until the outer pulp and juice fall away – work under a running hose. Or, soak entire dried leaf and shred down to get dried weavers. Wear rubber gloves – this causes a bad skin rash.	The dried wrinkled leaves can be sewn together to create container forms. Attached to the thorn at the tip is a strong fiber that runs down the center of the plant. This can be carefully cut out and used as a needle and thread. The fibers can also be twisted and plied to make cordage.
Fall and winter	Pull leaves at base or let them drop.	Great decorative heads – many colors.

MISCELLANEOUS

NAME	PART TO USE	CONDITION FOR USE	WHERE IT'S FOUND
Japanese Aralia (Fatsia)	Leaf stem	Dry until just pliable, then use immediately. Some dry brown stems will soak.	A landscaping plant.
Cast Iron Plant (Aspidistra)	Leaves – whole or split	Green or dry with soaking.	In gardens, also a house plant.
Giant Philodendron	Leaf sheaths – whole or split Roots Leaf stems – whole or split	Dry with soaking. Dry until barely flexible, then use immediately. Green or dry with soaking.	A landscape plant, try government, professional, and school buildings.
Papyrus – Umbrella Plant	Stem	Dry with minimal soaking.	Gardens
Bird of Paradise – Giant or Regular	Split stems Leaves	Green or dry with soaking.	Gardens – a tropical plant
Cymbidium Orchid	Leaves	Dry with soaking.	In a greenhouse, a tropical plant.
Horsetail Fern	Stems	Green or dry with soaking.	Any abandoned flat area.
Ferns – Boston Fern Sword Fern Maidenhair Fern Fiddle Head Fern	Stems – whole or split Roots	Dry with soaking.	Houseplants or tropicals or redwood forests, etc.

WHEN TO COLLECT	HOW TO COLLECT	SPECIAL INSTRUCTIONS
Any time – but can cut back really hard in the spring.	Pull stem at base.	Has a decorative head.
Any time – but fall and winter are best.	Cut leaf at base near stalk.	
Any time Fall and winter Any time	Pick up off of the ground. Cut the aerial root off next to the plant. Cut the stem at the base.	The leaf sheath is the red brown thing growing around the leaf when it's born. The sheath can be ironed flat between two damp towels for easier use or easier splitting. The dried leaves can be twisted into ropes.
Any time	Cut stem at base.	The three sided stem will need to be flattened.
Mature plants after flowering or when thinning.	Cut stem at base and split.	
any time – except when flowering.	Cut leaf at stem.	
Any time – but fall and winter are best.	Cut reproductive stalks at base – they're long and tall without branches.	To keep the dark green color, store them out of the sunlight.
Any time – but don't disturb the new growth – late June is best.	Cut stems at base – can be pruning. Find a root and dig after it – chop at plant. Be sparing.	Remove leaves by running hand from tip to base.

MISCELLANEOUS

NAME	PART TO USE	CONDITION FOR USE	WHERE IT'S FOUND
Fireweed	Stalks – whole or split	Green or dry with soaking.	Roadsides – generally considered a weed.
Fennel	Split stalks	Green – use just before it dries.	An herb garden
Ginger – many varieties	Leaves – twisted or cut	Dry with minimal soaking.	Gardens
Aristia	Leaves – split	Dry with soaking.	Gardens
Corn – Regular and Indian	Husks Leaves	Dry with soaking.	Corn fields. Grocery stores – packaged for tamales.

WHEN TO COLLECT	HOW TO COLLECT	SPECIAL INSTRUCTIONS
Late summer or fall	Cut at base or pull out of the ground.	The stalks are hollow — so when split you have the choice of a convex or concave surface.
Summer and fall	Cut stalk at base and split.	Odor remains.
When dry	Pick at base of leaf.	One variety in Hawaii remains pink when dry.
When leaves are dry — they will be black or charcoal grey.	Cut at base when dry.	Whole leaves can be used for imbrication.
Late summer and fall — any time in the grocery store.	Remove husks from corn ear and cut or pull leaves from stalk.	Lay husks out to dry completely in the sun — turn to bleach evenly.

Tendril Magic

by Doris Messick

Vine basketry is my first love. My inspiration and creativity are dependent on the wonderful twists and turns of wild vines; of which, grapevine is the most common. Grapevines grow in most parts of the United States, either wild or domesticated, and have those wonderful curly tendrils that all natural basket artists love. Unfortunately, in our area, grapevine harbors powderpost beetles and successfully resists all attempts at eradication. I hated to give up the tendrils, but the infected grapevine spread to my other vines and made basketry a constant losing battle.

A second blow to basketry came from a newly retired husband who wanted to travel. My basketry requires tubs and more tubs of soaking vines which, needless to say, do not travel well. I needed something small and portable that had the feel of the vines.

Grapevine tendrils have been the answer to my prayers. They have all the wonderful twists and curls that the vines do, just in miniature. They do *not* get buggy! In short, they travel well.

Judy Mulford, from Los Angeles, taught me looping (knotless netting) several years ago. She told me I only had to remember two things. I needed to be consistent, making my loops in one direction only -and- all the same size. I was unable to do that then, or now. But have found that, like with other naturals, it really doesn't matter.

The small size makes jewelry a natural. The tendril forms the framework, and, like vines, is easiest to shape when first harvested. They must the be dried so that any shrinkage will take place. Soaking the tendrils later permits a return to flexibility and the ability to shape a form.

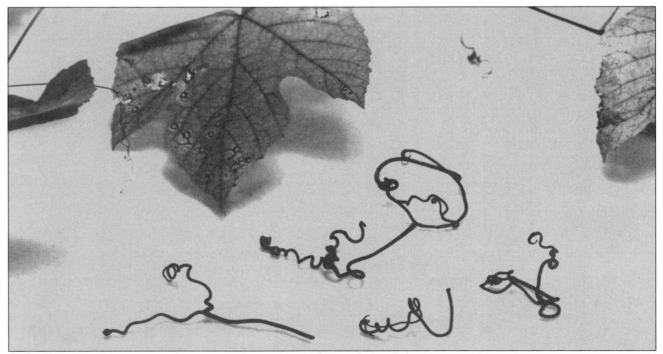

Grapevine and sample tendrils.

A simple enclosed shape, such as an oval or teardrop, is a good place to begin. Waxed linen is the easiest material to loop with. Metallic threads give a nice effect, but handle easier if first run through beeswax. The hardest to use, but most rewarding, are other vines. Possibilities include; morning glory, bind weed, or honeysuckle runners.

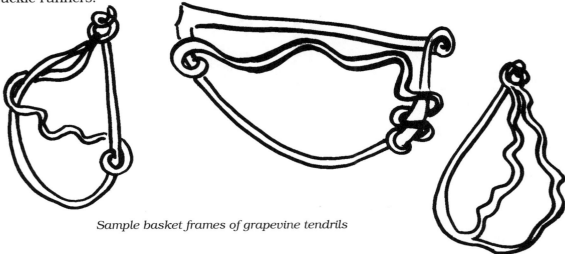

Sample basket frames of grapevine tendrils

Looping is simply the button hole or blanket stitch that my mother taught me when I was growing up. Anchor your thread at a joint and tie a knot. Unless you are working with wire or a vine, you will find it easiest to use a needle with a large eye. Tapestry, embroidery or yarn needles all work. Choose one that best suits *you and* that can handle the chosen size of thread.

I usually leave an end for future use or just to dangle. Go around the frame about 1/8" to 1/4" from the knot and come through the resulting loop.

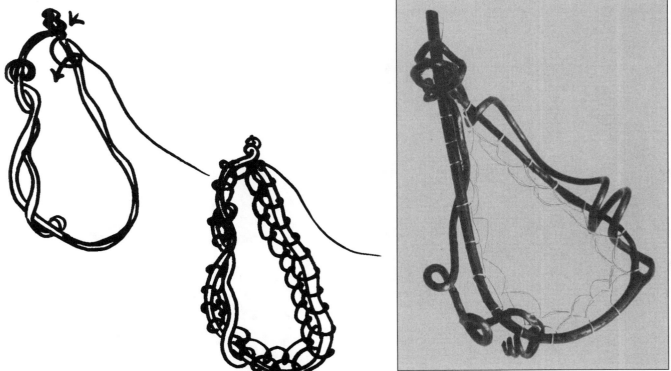

Repeat this simple step completely around the frame. Try different ways until you find which is the most comfortable for you. Your stitch can go either over or under the frame. You can go either to the left or right. The only necessary step is to go through the loop, which locks the stitch in place.

The second row of looping loops onto the first. Normal looping would call for one loop per (first row) loop.

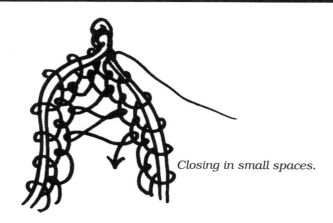

Closing in small spaces.

With irregular shapes, this will vary. Go with what comes naturally and fills the space. If one loop per loop makes the stitch too small, try skipping one at that point. (Usually this occurs on an inside corner.) If the stitch becomes too big, do two loops in one. The space changes with the shape of the tendril and the further away you get from the frame.

Continue looping for as many rows as needed. This will depend on the size of the frame, the thickness of your weaver, and the size of your stitches.

When the space becomes small, loop from one side to the other, filling in the space until you come to a wider section.

The center hole can be left open to form a *Dream Catcher*. To emphasize this, I do a final row of two stitches per loop. This helps the good dreams find their way through the hole; an important feature. Small dream catchers make earrings; larger ones can become pendants.

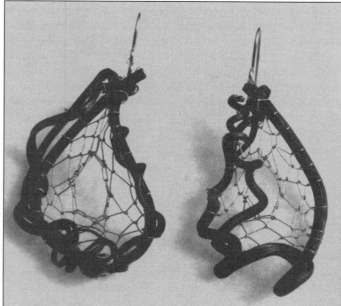

Tendril Earrings, looped, grapevine tendril and metallic thread, 1992.

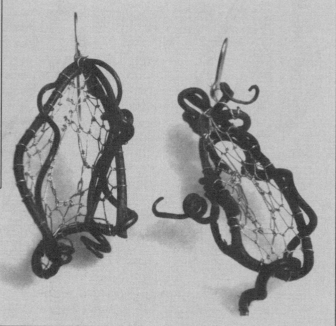

Tendril Earrings, looped, grapevine tendril and metallic thread, 1992.

Tendril Necklace, looped, grapevine tendril and waxed linen, 1.5" x 1.5" x 1", 1992.

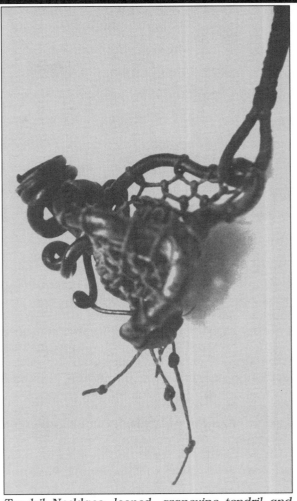

Tendril Necklace, looped, grapevine tendril and waxed linen, 1.5" x 1.5" x 1", 1992.

Miniature baskets can be formed from larger tendrils. Branched tendrils work best. The curly branches form the back and front of the basket, while the straight stem makes the bottom part. Many variations are possible. And more than one tendril can be used. More traditional baskets can be formed by leaving a small part of the grapevine as the top of the basket. The possibilities are limitless.

Looping becomes more complicated when forming a basket. Start by going around the entire top rim. The second row will show which areas need to be filled in and what direction to take to fill in the basket shape. No two are alike, so I can't give you specifics. Experiment. If it doesn't look right, take out the necessary stitches and try again. Don't hesitate to change directions or go back and forth in one area. It's the results that count; not how you get there.

Most baskets require two lengths of weavers. It doesn't pay to work with a weaver that's too long. It just gets knotted, worn and tired looking. I always try to start and end at the same spot, leaving the ends dangling for effect. Beads or other dangles can be added if desired.

Cords can be added to make necklaces, either of waxed linen, leather or synthetic cord. Earring findings are available at any craft store. Jump rings, normally used to attach earrings, do not adapt well to the irregular tendrils. Fine wire twisted with needle nosed pliers allows you to make an attachment that permits the earring to hang properly.

The best part is that each one is unique. There is no boring repetition. They are fun to make and fun to wear. Be creative in miniature! Be creative as you travel! Gather those tendrils and loop away the hours. Most of all, have fun!

Sculptural Knotless Netting

by Sally Santosuosso

If you are intrigued by creative problem solving, may I entice you to the joys of knotless netting? All that you need is a discerning eye, a willingness to gamble with occasional failure, and a bit of flexibility.

Knotless netting (looping) is one of my favorite techniques because its versatility makes it useful in many forms of fiber art, i.e. basketry, sculpture, embroidery, needleweaving and jewelry. Like most *bag-lady* fiber artists, I am attracted to the hunt for the perfect material. Since knotless netting stretches in all directions, I generally look for strong, non-elastic, yet flexible, materials to use as looping strands. Cotton twine, waxed/unwaxed linen, raffia, thin round reed, flat cane and wire are wonderful stock items for knotless netting — especially for those of you who combine media or alter the characteristics of your materials through overpainting, dyeing, or stiffening.

Wire, in particular, gives immeasurable freedom for establishing structural soundness, without heaviness, because it bends easily and holds its shape. It also adapts to any part of the netting process; the working strand or the foundation support. A quick glance at the following lists will give you an idea of some of your resources for collecting wire and other suitable structural supports.

Veil of Hope, knotless netting, mixed media (synthetic fibers, metal filter, beads and wire, 1992.

Wire Sources: Hardware, craft and yarn stores, electrical or plumbing supply houses, antique stores, flea markets, radio/TV/, computer stores, garden centers, close out stores, fishing/marine outlets, and telephone companies.

Wire Types: Coated telephone and computer wires (available in multicolor), galvanized steel wire, coated steel wire, copper wire, single and multi-stranded (twisted) electrical wire, coated and uncoated florist wire, beading wire (green, silver, gold colors), picture frame wire (slightly heavier, often stranded), coat hangers, and other found (wire) objects.

Wire thickness is measured by the gauge. Gauges are designated by numbers, the larger the number, the thinner and softer the wire.

For knotless netting, I prefer 18 to 20 gauge wire. Its thickness provides good structure without jeopardizing pliability, but your wire choice will depend on the size and nature of your project.

Other Materials: Round reed, vine rattan, koboo and poulet rattan, wild vines, paper fiber core, plastic tubing, copper and other metal rods, and recycled wire forms (wheels, lamp shades, wire nursery containers).

Building Supports: I am amazed at how many potential art forms are waiting to be discovered among found objects. Look for items that provide free lines, patterns, or even ready made shapes. Armed only with a sharp pair of wire cutters, needle nose pliers, a large tapestry needle, thread, and an active imagination, it will be easy to uncover wonderful structures.

Building Supports — The Process

Any method for permanently affixing sides is acceptable *if* it holds securely and does not detract from the total design. I use plastic bag ties to temporarily secure wire elements until a final design has been solidified. Then I either lash the sides together or join them with wrapping or repeated larks head knots.

Sometimes the sides pin together to create a single shape. Other times, forms emerge as multiple planes.

Whenever found objects or vines are used as supports, they require the removal of extraneous lines in order to maintain simplicity. Whatever the case, foundation supports will ultimately set the direction for the basket or sculpture, and will hold the first row of looping. Sometimes, however, looping begins on itself.

History — A Definition

Although we will explore only simple looping, there are many wonderful variations that can be found in various books and publications. My favorite references for knotless netting and needleweaving are Needlelace and Needleweaving by Jill Nordfors and Design Principles and Fiber Techniques by Joan Michaels Paque. The Paque book is an exhaustive workbook of all fiber techniques.

Keep in mind that although simple work may be enhanced texturally by fancy variations, sculptural forms often Have stronger visual impact if only simple looping is used. Before you begin, I encourage you to reflect on the intent of your piece.

The basic process of knotless netting utilizes a single continuous working strand to form rows of interconnected loops. Limitless in its appearance, knotless netting is not only net-like, but tightly controlled, resembling cloth or even built up on itself to become both texture and form.

Although it is being revived as a creative technique for contemporary fiber artists, simple looping is one of the oldest and most universal of all fiber techniques. It has been widely used throughout history to meet the functional and decorative needs of all cultures. There have been many names to describe the same stitch, i.e., *needlelace, brussels stitch, half-hitch, looping* and many more. Even variations have specific names. Despite the name changes, each application uses the same basic structure.

Basic Looping — The Process

This structure begins by cutting a flexible piece of material into a comfortable, but practical length. Although it is easier to hide and rejoin threads at the ends of rows rather than within, too long a strand can be a tangled disaster. Anticipating when a thread will run out is often a great time-saver.

The first looping strand must be attached to a support, such as an armature, cloth, or simply a temporary holding cord, which is removed when the project is finished. The method of joining the first working strand is called a *reverse larks head*. The larks head should be longer on the right side to accommodate looping from left to right.

Follow the steps listed below to understand simple looping. Directions cover basic looping, working in one direction, from left to right, as well as working back and forth.

Article photo credit: Roger Olney

Working in One Direction Only (Left to Right):

1. The working strand swings over the holding strand.
2. It goes behind the holding strand and down through the loop it just made.
3. Continue to make loops, working towards the right) until a desired row is achieved.

4. To begin a new row, place each successive loop into the middle curve of the row above it. Most baskets and other three dimensional work are looped in one direction only, from left to right, but they may also work in both directions.

Working in Both Directions

1. Complete the first row as described above, working from left to right.

2. To reverse directions, make an "S" curve at the end of the first row and reverse the procedure. Notice the appearance of the loops when they move back and forth. They also lie in opposite direction to the rows above and below. Flat work uses either method, depending upon whether or not it can be worked from both the front and back sides.

Circular Looping

Circular shapes are a bit different. Some have separate structural supports *but* use the same wire (material) for both the holding strand and working strand. A single strand forms a circle that leaves a small tale of wire to the left and a long strand to the right. The long strand can make loops around the circle in the same manner as previously described.

When enough loops are placed on the support to create the desired circular opening, the short tale is pulled gently. This closes up the circle. Successive rows are looped into the preceding rows.

Anyone who wishes to distort the shape can do so by increasing or decreasing the amount of loops per row. The creative potential of this technique is limited only to the extent of your vision. It uses the same design elements of line, color, rhythm, spatial relationship and shape as any other fine art. Lets explore some of them.

Two More Looping Styles

The first one works through the previous loop. The second one works around/behind the previous loop.

Over Flow, knotless netting and sprayed pulp paper, mixed media, 4" x 7" x 14", 1992.

Another view

Line

Knotless netting is a linear technique which builds up forms, line by line, loop by loop, layer by layer. Think of the working strand as a textural line, sketching and shading as it flows in and out of space. What are its characteristics? Is it a sturdy wire line? A fragile fiber line? What quality attracts you?

Though characteristically a technique for creating open work, tightly netted structures work just as well. Their density is controlled by the size of the loops, the size and type of the materials, how tightly the loops are pulled, and how far apart they are spaced.

Color

Sometimes looping involves color changes. If you are careful with placement, the looped transition will be as smooth as that found in tapestry weaving. Once the netting builds up, you can easily camouflage joinings and endings within the body. Here are some suggestions for manipulating color:

1. Float contrasting color on the inside, pulling strands forward as desired. Larks head knots may be added anywhere on a row.

2. Loop with several colors at once, separating individual colors at will.

3. Deliberately expose ends.

4. Alter color by painting or dyeing.

Space

Success in netted basketry and other fiber forms depends in part on interesting spatial relationships. Usually the viewer notices inner, outer, filled and empty spaces, each playing an integral part in the total design. My methods for balancing space include:

1. Single/simultaneous looping with materials of different weight, thickness and type.

2. Overlapping layers of single or multi-netted structures.

3. Varying size and looseness of the loops and the space between them.

4. Changing directions, contrasting solid vs. open spaces.

5.. Adding textural embellishments

6. Knotting joinings, allowing knots to become decorative textural interests.

Ending and Joining

Sometimes joinings should not show. Some of the ways to camouflage endings are:

1. Splice materials whenever possible by unraveling both old and new ends, then re-twist them with the aid of clear fabric glue.

2. Tie old and new ends with a *weaver's knot*, placing it in an inconspicuous spot where ends can be hidden by new or previously made loops. The weavers knot is strong, allowing for closely clipped ends. Gluing is still advisable.

3. Hide an overhand knot with a bead or similar embellishment.

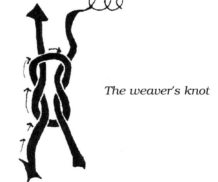

The weaver's knot

Finally, looped forms may be transformed by altering the materials through painting, beading, stitching or weaving. Any combination of media that furthers your imagery is worthwhile.

A friend once said "Art should grab you in the gut, and appeal to a part of you far beyond a surface level." This statement challenges basket artists and fiber artists to look farther than solid design or fined tuned skills to develop forms that reverently communicate who you are and what is important to you. Then, I believe, the integrity of your work will elicit such a response in others.

What motivates you as an artist? How does your process affect your art work? How do you strike a balance between technique and vision?

March of the Pink Flamingos, random weave, reed, paint, beads, plastic bags, wire and plastic flamingos, 8" x 7" x 6", 1992.

Nancy Goes

Basket for L and M, U know Who U R, random weave, reed, paint and mixed media, 10" x 9" x 13", 1992.

B.D. Massey

Crying for a Vision, plaster gauze, vines, twigs and bark, 3' x 3' x 5', 1991. Photo credit: Rick Zaiden.

Ankaret Dean

Skywalk, nylon rope, metal rods and natural materials, 90' x 6', Owen Sound, Canada, 1992.

Dawn MacNutt

Blue Madonna, twined willow cast in bronze, 1992.

Over the past decade I've worked to achieve freestanding woven sculpture in enduring materials. On loom weaving was somewhat restrictive in terms of form. Seeing my dilemma, Jack Larsen recommended basketry techniques to me on several occasions. Ultimately, the suggestion *took*, and I succumbed to the charms of twining and interlacing in some of its myriad forms. Basketry and weaving are wonderful occupations. Primarily, though, for me they are means to an end. That end is to create forms Usually human forms. Sometimes trees. Mainly human forms. Containers of the human soul.

Photo credit: Peter Barss

The mood of the figures is usually ambiguous; somewhat abstract; sometimes somber, sometimes contemplative, sometimes joyous. Rather than expressing specific personal feelings, I think my work reveals vulnerability, which opens the viewer to their own personal responses and feelings. The natural consequence of marrying the casting technique with woven and interlaced work is that fragmentation during the process is easily achieved. I have exploited the technique to portray the beauty of human frailty. There is poetry in the parts left out. Not much has been written about the partial figure. A fine book by Albert Elsen is published by the Baltimore Museum of Art: The Partial Figure in Modern Sculpture. Reading about sculpture, however, has been secondary to experiencing it. I take every opportunity to see sculpture of all kinds. And to touch it when possible. Touching sculpture is very important, I think. That is another reason I like to use enduring materials in woven and interlaced work. Sculpture, like baskets, begs to be touched. Have you ever seen a basket you didn't want to touch?

Doing the work has some sensual pleasures too: shaping wetted willow into elegant rounded shapes; flowing with the pliancy of fresh vines; smelling the fragrance of seagrass; shaping woven wire socks into shapely hollow limbs; enjoying the faint smell of fresh sweat, more pungent from the exertion completing the difficult piece; and the satisfaction when the piece *sits* the way you hoped it would.

I certainly feel passionately about the *subject matter* of my work. It is often as not about someone dear and precious to me who is experiencing something traumatic. However, as the work progresses, the piece often shifts and changes in subtle ways; it often reveals something new and unknown as it grows. That is part of the excitement of doing the work.

Maybe art is *peculiar perception*. If we are true to our own inner self, the way in which each of us manifests our vision is unique. Forgetting the siren call of approval from others is a freeing, empowering experience. When we can forget about sale, commission or exhibition, some magical things happen. We can't forget about sales, commission and exhibition and still expect to eat. But saving some parts of ourselves for pure exploration is like saving the frosting for the last. We mustn't wait until it dries out.

Courage, twined palm inflorescenes cast in bronze, 19" x 7" x 6", 1992.

Imagery

by Judy Mulford

My life centers around my family. Being a wife, mother and grandmother have been the most important things in my life. So, it is quite natural for me to use basketry to focus on the areas I know and love the most. My baskets honor and celebrate the family unit.

I have been making baskets or over fifteen years. At first I was enamored with the materials and the fact that I could actually create a basket. I was intrigued with pine needles and spent years making semi-traditional and non-functional baskets. Then I decided I wanted my baskets to become more than visually pretty. I wanted my baskets to say something — to have content. I didn't want to just make s*ale* baskets, I wanted to make *soul* baskets.

The process was slow and scary. I realized that this creative gift I had been given was also a valuable tool I could use to help me work out emotional problems or life passages. The images at first were abstract, but I knew what they meant. Combining clay with pine needles enabled me to sculpt my own images, and, to make bases for my pine needle coiling. The bases were slab built clay that I pressed into my own pots and pans and imprinted with my mother's handwoven cloth. My mother, who died in 1970, then became apart of each piece. At first I made clay lids of cats, dogs, lizards and rabbits for my coiled baskets. These images were *safe* and not controversial.

Feline Fetish, coling, clay, pine needles, waxed linen, dye, wax and paint, 5.5" x 4" x 4.5", 1986.

I"m 50 and I'm Glad, I think, coiling, clay, pine needles, raffia, beads, wax and dye, 8.5" x 13", 1988.

Then I began to use more and more female figures. They became more personal, autobiographical and graphic. I made large baskets with small figures and large figures with small baskets. The titles became important and humor evolved. Slowly I gravitated into <u>only</u> making pieces that contained imagery focusing on the family, motherhood and grandmotherhood.

By this time my figures had become stylized (I use a lot of rusty nails and rusty, run over bottle caps) and I began dressing my figures with looped, back pack pouches holding babies. I LOVED the looping (knotless netting) technique and began using it to cover entire pieces. Even though my materials and technique had changed from coiling with pine needles to looping with waxed linen, the images were still the same and the pieces were still dark and heavy and had a feeling of antiquity.

Basket Maker with head Dress, looping and coiling, clay, waxed linen, pine needles, paper, beads and wax, 6" x 9.5", 1989.

Mother and Child, looping, clay, waxed linen, leather, nails and beads, 6" x 17", 1991`.

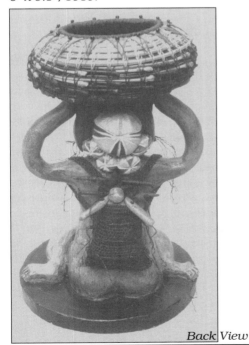

Back View

Back View

During the last few years I have taken another major artistic step. I let go of my pine needles and have allowed myself to go forward and grow with the looping technique. For me, this versatile and ancient technique is very symbolic because it is also the button hole stitch which is historically rooted with woman's work in the home.

Now my work is even more autobiographical, personal, graphic and narrative. Instead of clay for this format, I use gourds as a base to integrate my photo images, drawings, script and babies in pouches. These are my *Baby Baskets*. Each basket comes with two extra babies in case one is lost. (Just like when you buy an expensive, new dress or jacket, you get extra buttons.)

The titles are also important for the pieces…"The Family," "Passages," "The Nurturer, The Early Years," "Alone, The Empty Nest," "So Many Roles/ So Little Time," and my favorite, "By the Skin of My Neck" (You know you are getting older when you pick up your grandson and instead of him putting his arm AROUND your neck, he holds onto the skin ON your neck).

Note: My maternal grandmother made dolls, my mother was a loom weaver, and my father is a sculptor and painter. My pieces reflect the talents that they have shared with me.

So Many Roles/So Little Time, looping, gourd, waxed linen, raffia, polyform, burning and dye, 10.5" x 6.5", 1992. Collection of Rosemary Fields, courtesy of ProArt.

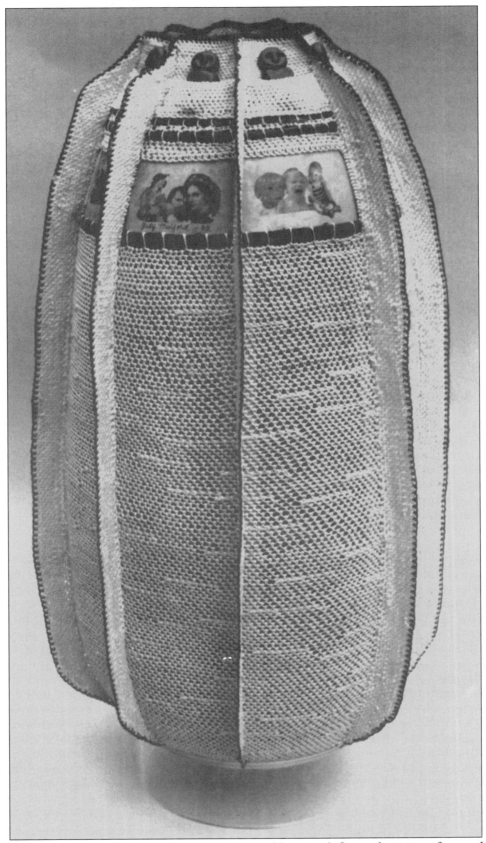

By the Skin of My Neck, looping, gourd, waxed linen, polyform, photo transfers and dyed pandanus, 8.75" x 15.5", 1992. Collection of Jane Lander, courtesy of ProArt.

Joanna Lindsly

In mother's house, years of family crafts were all around us — the 1828 sampler of Zibiah Corson, age nine, the Kansas grandma's embroidered tea towels, the Oklahoma grandmother's painted china, great-grandma's quilts. By 1890, everyone in the family had also gotten their hands on a camera and enthusiastically *shot* everything in sight. For 100 years they filled album after album with personal history.

Working within basketry, I try to reconcile their photos, diaries and letters with my collection of antique postcards and to record and preserve the everyday history of ordinary people, and the friends, relative, children and pets of yesterday.

1919: Johnny Came Marching Home, coiling, embroidery floss, reed, hand dyed raffia, photocopies from family albums, 48 star flag, and cotton doll pattern, 9" x 8", 1991. *

Sunny Southern California, coiling, reed, raffia and antique post-cards, 8" x 5.5", 1991. Photo credit: Ben Janken.

*Photo credit: Gabriel Moulin Studios.

Chinatown, USA, coiling, reed, raffia, photocopies, antique postcards with a brass finial and teak stand, 6" x 9", 1990. Photo credit and copyright: Gabriel Moulin Studios.

A Kansas Woman, coiling, cotton fabric, hand dyed raffia, reed, photocopies from family albums and Fiber Flex, 7.5" x 12.5", 1991.*

Leah Danberg

Dreams Change, knotting, waxed linen and embroidery floss, 5.75" x 4.25" x 3.5", 1992.

Keep Testing Reality, knotting, waxed linen and embroidery floss, 6.5" x 4.25" x 4.25", 1992.

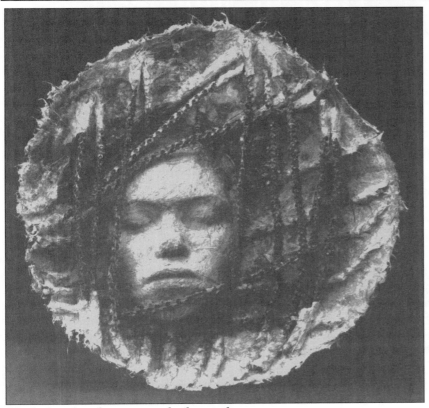

Mask, handmade paper and nikau palm, 15" dia, 1992.

Willa Rodgers

Photo credit: Lynne Griffith

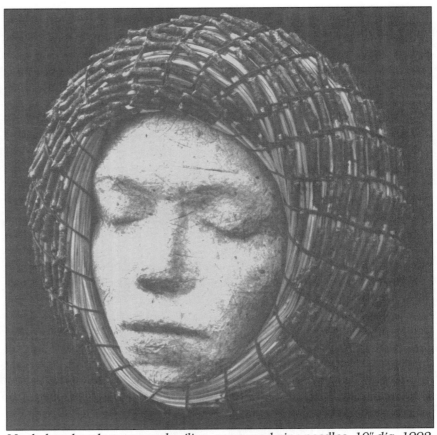

Mask, handmade paper and coiling, paper and pine needles, 10" dia, 1992.

Just Another Mid-Life Crisis

by Marilyn Moore

"All right Mom, we have to talk. I need to register for school in the fall and I need to see a counselor over there. Will you come over with me? In fact, you have been talking about going back to school for as long as I can remember, why don't you come with me and we'll register together?" Kara, my oldest daughter, who had graduated from high school that spring (1989), presented a good argument. I had always longed to go back to school and finish my education. I had started college right out of high school and like many people, my social life and lack of enthusiasm for school, got in the way of actually accomplishing anything there. Later came marriage and children, a divorce and another marriage, all of which took up more time and energy. School became something I kept putting off. As I thought about Kara's words, it seemed that she was right and time had come to do something about this dream. My basketry career made me happy. The progress I had made with what I could learn from my own experiments, and what I could pick up in workshops and conferences, was satisfactory, but I still felt that lack of education. Some of the skills which being an artist, teacher and author required were also missing. Maybe she was right, maybe it was time. Trina, my youngest daughter, was still in high school, but she was busy with her own life, and didn't require as much attention anymore. Maybe it was time to focus on myself and my personal growth.

Vestige, coiled, pine needles and raffia, 6" x 11" dia, 1986-88.

Tribute, coiled, waxed linen and polished hemp, 9" x 10.5" dia, 1991-92.

Article photo credit: John L. Moore.

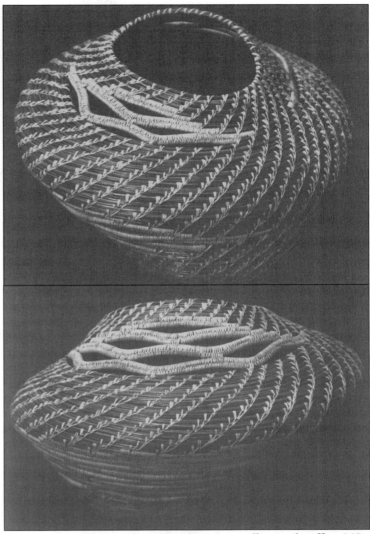

Resistance, coiled and wrapped, pine needles and raffia, 11" x 10.5" x 8", 1988.

As I eased my way back into school (I only took one class that first quarter), I realized the changes that were happening in my life were not always the ones that I expected. Not having as much time for housework was predictable, but my personal life changed drastically as well. I no longer had time for leisurely phone conversations, and lunches with my friends. I became very focused on school and studying. Not only did I have less energy for socializing I didn't have as much time for basketry either. Volunteer time and guild activities also disappeared. Mid-life is a difficult time for both men and women, as I became more aware of this I realized that I had added an extra element to an already confusing and unsettling time. I love school however, and for a while it was one of the few sane things in my life, an anchor I could hold onto. As problems with rebellious teenagers, elderly parents and money threatened to take over, I became more and more grateful that school was a part of my life.

My art work has also changed dramatically. The personal growth from exploring new techniques and design principles, and new areas of study that held no interest for me before, have also influenced my work. Classes that I've taken like math, economics and anthropology have all made a difference in my art work, as well as the art classes. Where technique and form held my interest before, color, design, symbolism and growth are beginning to creep into my work. My baskets were two toned explorations of form and pattern and now I have introduced color and new techniques into them as well.

Then I took a pottery class to see if I could explore mixed media in my work. It changed how I looked at vessels forever. In that class I also made a plaster mold of my own face. That started an interest in making life masks of myself. Now I'm exploring the meaning behind the different masks I wear everyday. This is one way that I have incorporated more of myself into my work. Even though this latest work is still immature in technique and style, it is still another step in my growth as an adult female who is looking for her own identity, separate from her husband, children and parents. It is a time of tremendous artistic and personal growth for me.

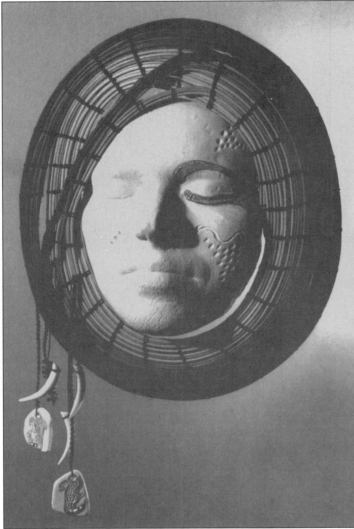

Tribal Series: Dreaming Woman, cast clay and coiled, porcelain, reed, waxed linen and beads, 2.5" x 9" x 13.5", 1992.

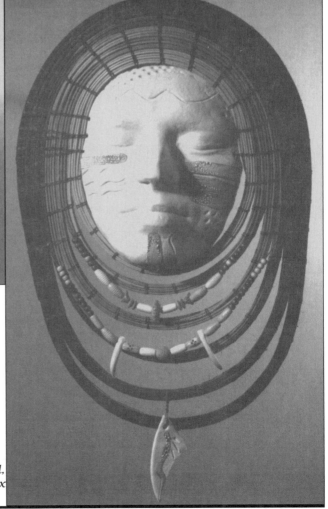

Tribal Series: Shaman's Vision, cast and coiled, porcelain, reed, waxed linen and beads, 2.25" x 9" x 15.5", 1992.

I Will See No Evil, cast and coiled, porcelain, reed, waxed linen, beads and copper wire, 2.25" x 8.75" x 12.5", 1991.

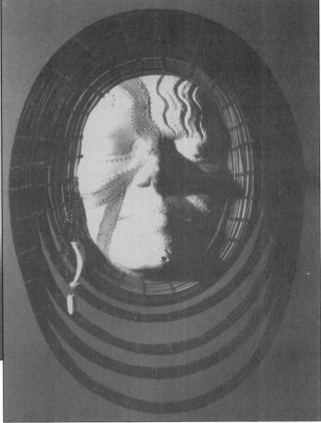

Tribal Series: Earth Mother, cast and coiled, porcelain, reed, waxed linen and beads, 3" x 9.5" x 13", 1992.

As I look to the future, wondering where will I go with this new direction in my life, I ask myself "What does my life hold after school?" The answer to this question is "Only to the extent that I limit my imagination." I want to continue to make my art, including baskets which have become such an important part of my life. I enjoy teaching what I have learned and in the same vein, writing has become more interesting as well. Maybe there will be a book in my future. Even at middle age it is exciting to contemplate what I will be when I grow up.

As I begin my fourth year in community college (yes I'm going slowly) I realize that I have taken almost all of the classes that I can at this school and soon I will have to transfer to a University. I have become more and more careful of the classes which I take as the probability of a degree becomes more real. When I started I had no real goal in mind, but it becomes more defined each day. The possibilities are endless.

Going to school every day, I walk across campus and there's Trina, my youngest daughter who has now also started college. I look at her and see another fellow student who has grown up into a lovely young adult. I'm grateful that as I let go of her emotionally, and of that time when her life and her sister's life depended on me, I find more of my own time and space. The growth that I have seized and the opportunities which are mine are all part of the next adventure in my life — which has already begun. I look to the future with a newly found confidence and pride in what I have accomplished.

Marcia Rhodes

Detail

Photo credit: Abraham's Photographic Studios

The container form has deep spiritual meaning for me and my fascination with it has held me willingly captive for many years. I'm fortunate to live in an era which supports the notion of the fiber vessel being a medium of expression that has the potential for reflecting the most profound insights and longings of the container's maker. My own container forms are pathways for searching — not just for new shapes and unique combination of materials, but for deep significance and courage to accept what life has in store for me.

I've chosen autobiographical themes recently as a way of celebrating the companionship and legacy of those who have influenced me. My recent *Memory Pouches* that honor the spirit and courage of both my natural mother and a special woman who has been like a mother to me, materialized not so much from a desire to sustain the memory of my experience beyond my own lifetime. Instead, in the way that rich soil gives birth to new life forms, I incorporated soil and mulch as well as ancestors into the handmade paper to acknowledge my roots and express appreciation for my origins.

I like working at the edge of chaos where the creative process is most vibrant for me. It often happened during the assembly of the *Memory Pouches* that too much paint here or too sharp and image there unexpectedly threatened to ruin the subtle outcome. Them my ideas about how things were supposed to be were challenged and transformed as I tapped into a deeper layer of perception beyond my rational mind. Like the traditional North American Indian basket artist who knew how to express the intellectual spiritual aspirations of her life and in whose hands objects of beauty found great expression in form, color and design, I strive to create works of love as vehicles to embody my personal mythology, my own folklore — even my prayers.

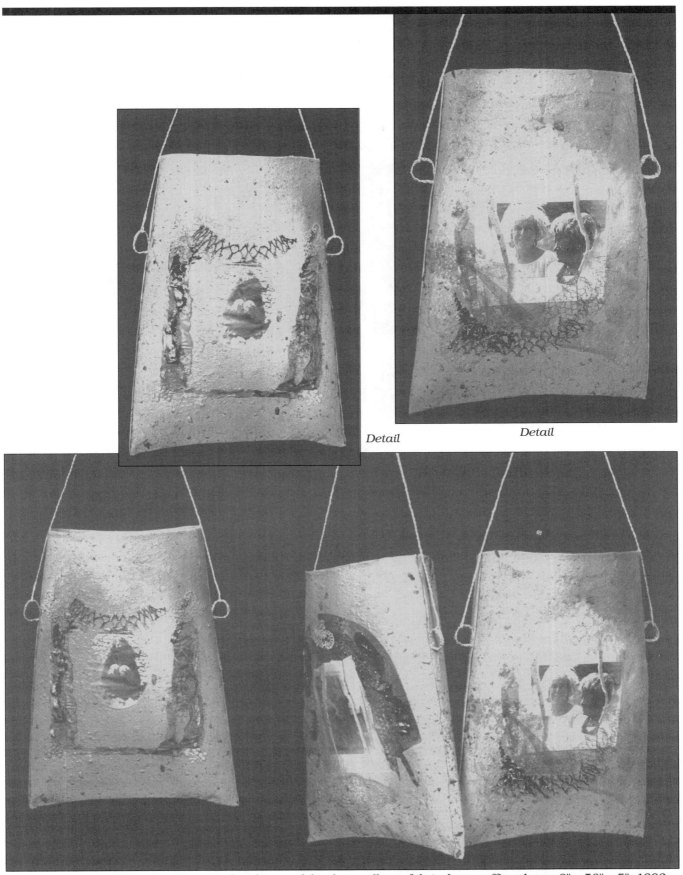

Detail

Detail

Memory Pouches, Handmade paper, beadws, mulch, photo collage, fabric, lace, raffia, abaca, 9" x 50" x 5", 1992.

Stoney Ridge

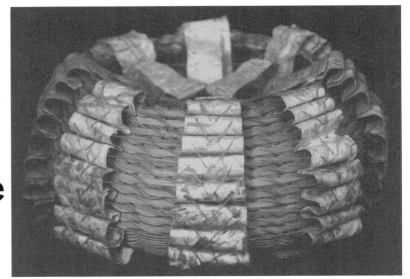

Side View

d'acqua Lily, twined, T-twined and stitched, reed, handmade paper and pearl cotton,
12" x 12" x 6", 1992.

Photo credit: Janine Collins

Flo Hoppe

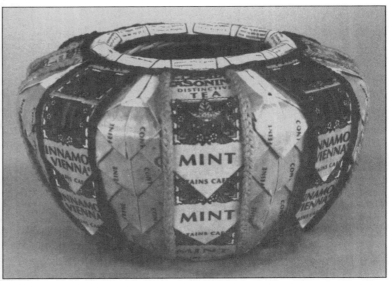

Tea For Quite A Few, twining, paper folding and braiding, rattan, tea bag envelopes, cotton and linen, 6" x 6" x 4", 1991.

Cheveux, twining and sumi-e, rattan, paper and ink, 4.5" x 4" x 17", 1991.

Photo credit: John C. Keys

Mary Merkel-Hess

I've lived my life in the American Midwest and I am immersed in this particular place. I am fond of the landscape and the prairies and grasses are the subject of my work. It is a landscape of sweeping horizontals broken by the upright verticals of growing things. A landscape whose rigid geometry of fields and rows dissolved into thickets and ditches. The cottonwoods in my backyard seem as majestic as mountains to me. There is not color I haven't found in the sky; no shape not growing somewhere in my garden.

Baskets can embody a range of human emotion and lately I look for the whimsical as well as the serious. Baskets haven't said everything they can say yet. I think there is more to do.

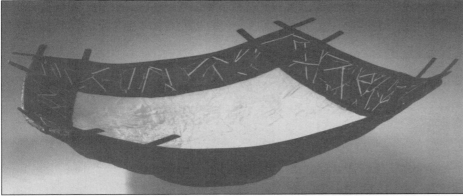

Summer Light, paper and reed, 5" x 17" x 17", 1989.

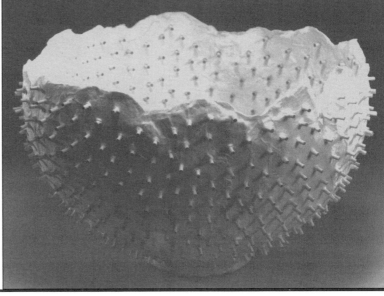

Seed Head, molded paper, paper and wood, 12" x 12" x 8", 1989.

Sagittal, molded paper, paper and paper cord, 30" x 18" x 26", 1992.

Thistle, molded paper, paper and paper cord, 22" x 10" x 10", 1991.

Tall Grass, molded paper, paper and paper cord, 20" x 6" x 26", 1991.

Pam Barton

Grecianesque, handmade paper: sheets, cast, dyed, spun and twined, and twining, paper, raffia and dye, 9" x 10" x 8.5", 1992.

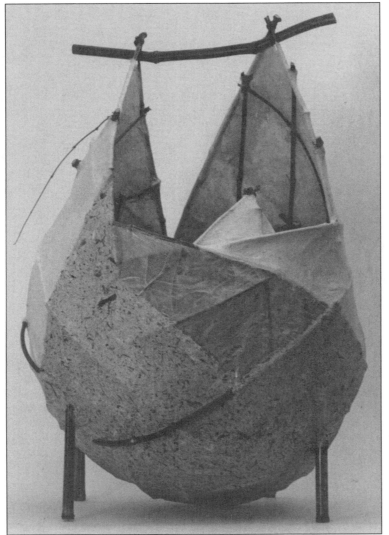

Photo credit: Sheri Siegel

Yume No Su (Nest of Dreams), random weave and cast paper, black bamboo, handmade paper, hog gut and waxed linen, 12" x 15" x 23", 1992.

Betz Salmont

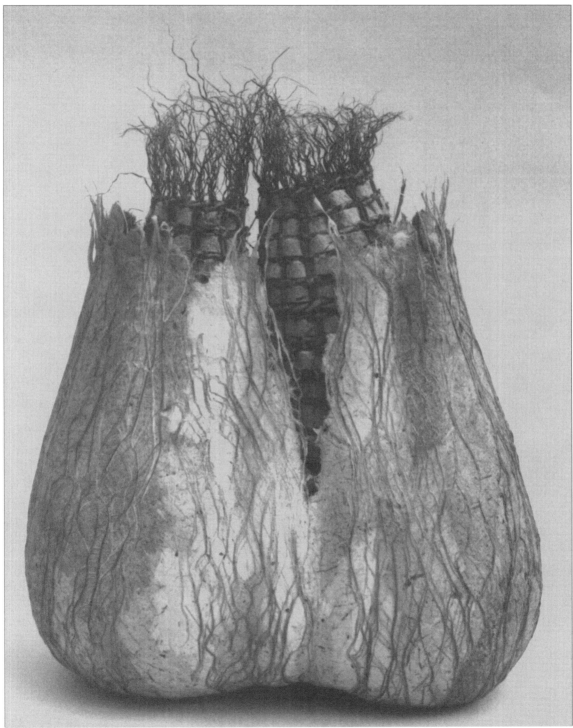

Birth of A Basket II, cast and woven, handmade paper, dracaena and palm infloresences; paper made of banana fiber, bamboo sheaths, abaca and kozo, 11.5" x 7" x 14", 1992. From the collection of Joan Borinstein.

Elisabeth Schuman

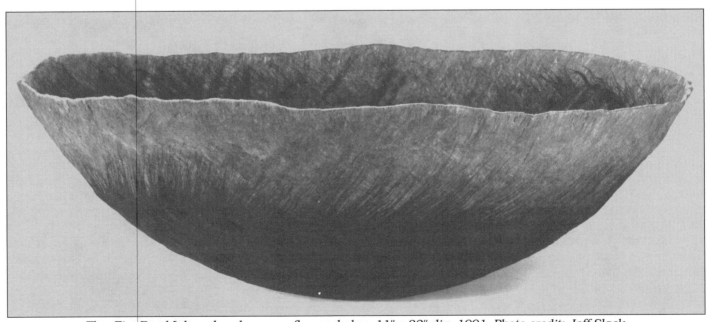

Flax Fire Bowl I, hamdmade paper, flax and glue, 11" x 32" dia, 1991. Photo credit: Jeff Slack

Gammy Miller

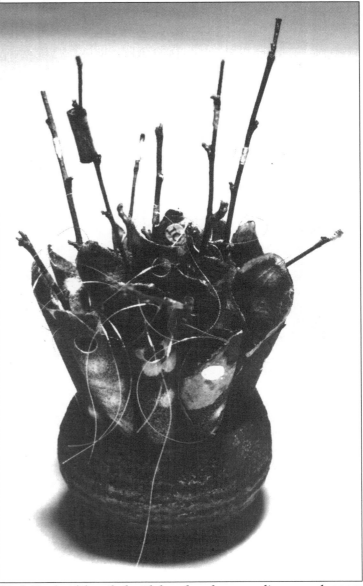

Spirographus Basket, coiled, linen, mud, paper and grapevine, 3.5" x 3" x 4.5", 1992. (Spirographus is a kind of deep sea fan worm.)

Photo credit: Ken Kimerling

Birch Basket (1), coiled with handmade paper, linen, mud, paper and birch, 3" x 3" x 6", 1992.

Jo Stealey

Having been trained as a potter as well as a weaver, I came to basketry through a love of vessels as well as textiles. The paper vessels began with a workshop in papermaking about 10 years ago; I was hooked. Paper provided me with a malleable material, much like clay, which would also produce the bright colors I sought. I could cast the paper, stitch it or cover an armature with this material. It synthesized the diversity of materials and techniques I had used in my work up to that point.

My vessels are sculptural expressions of events in my life, as well as physical representations of my connection with the elements of nature. The shapes and surface designs hearken to rituals from the past as well as those currently present in my life. Themes often involve aspects of the environment such as *Vortex to Extinction*. Although whimsical in appearance, the piece is a visual statement of our environment in crisis. We are on the edge of extinction; environmental balance must be addressed immediately.

Turtle Woman Basket represents the Native American custom of making a wedding basket for the bride to be. The basket was meant to adorn her home as a nonfunctional symbol of long life, prosperity and happiness. Thus the ritualistic presence and formal qualities of the piece. *Eek! Eek! There's a Snake On My Steps* records a momentous visit of a rattlesnake on the steps of my studio. *Dawn*, as the name implies, was inspired by a memory of the rising sun.

Eek! Eek! There's A Snake On My Steps, handmade paper, cotton and abaca, sticks, thread and paint, 6" x 6" x 15", 1991.

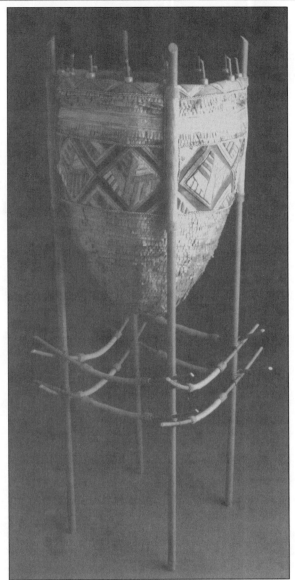

Turtle Woman Basket, twining, reed, paper, waxed linen and paint, 10" x 10" x 36", 1991.

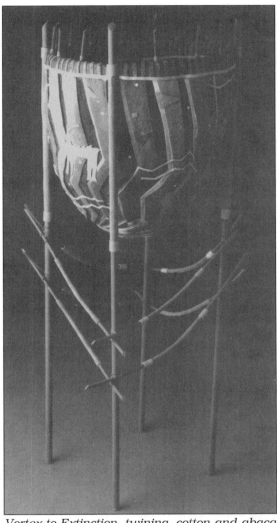

Vortex to Extinction, twining, cotton and abaca paper, reed, dowels and paint, 12" x 12"x 36", 1991.

The techniques I use are varied and call on the many media and experiences I've had over the years. I begin by making paper from cotton, flax, abaca, kozo or other plant fibers. An armature is often twined out of reed to form the base. The piece is then covered with paper, much as a two-dimensional collage artist would.

Dawn was produced by a technique I call "shag," created by cutting larger pieces of paper into small pieces and gluing them to the armature — a time consuming process to say the least. Other times, the vessel shape is cast from a mold, either found or made from plaster.

A third method I use to form pieces is to begin with flat sheets of paper and collage elements on to them (i.e. *Eek! Eek! There's a Snake On My Steps)*. Once the collage is finished, the pieces are stitched on a sewing machine to create the three-dimensional shape.

Linings and messages on the interior of the pieces provide an integral part of the overall message. It often contains the essence of the piece's statement. As a basket artist I am making containers of space and the volume. Because of this, the piece must be equally interesting on the inside as well as out. Thus a vortex on the inside of *Vortex to Extinction*, a turtle on the inside of *Turtle Woman Basket*, and a screaming woman on the interior of *Eek! Eek! There's a Snake On My Steps*.

Dawn, twining with overlay, reed and cotton and abaca paper, 8" x 8" x 18", 1991.

Substituting Handmade Paper for Bark

by Terry M. Greenstein

Bark containers and baskets have always fascinated me. They are often very simple in construction yet elegant in design. The material gives an implied strength because of it's natural origin and at the same time it provides one with a glimpse into it's past life. Bark, does however, have some limitations for me as a basket artist. The first, and foremost, is that in order to work with bark, one must have an abundant supply of trees. I use the word *abundant* because I don't believe in destroying our environment to satisfy our need for raw materials. I live in the suburbs outside of Boston and the trees around us are cherished for the beauty they contribute to our surroundings. The other limitation is the narrow color range one has when working with bark. Color is very important in my work and has often been the motivating element in a piece. About a year ago, I realized I could create bark-like vessels without using bark — by utilizing handmade paper.

For the past four years many of the containers I've created have been paper. In recent years I have used the pulp spraying technique to produce paper. Some of my vessels have been sprayed directly onto a form and have a very organic look to them, whereas others have been formed from sheets of paper. The concept of substituting paper for bark came to me one winter. I realized that pulp sprayed paper sheets are similar to bark in their texture, and, that paper can be treated like a piece of bark. The forms I had always admired could now be created from handmade paper.

The colored pulp is sprayed directly onto a canvas. The paper side that touches the canvas is smooth, like inner bark and the outer side is very textural, like outer bark. In addition to creating a bark-like material, another exciting feature of pulp spraying is that the paper is similar to a pointillist painting. All of the different colors that are placed next to each other, and on top of each other, create new colors.

When working with bark, there are many varieties of trees to work with and each produces a different appearance and effect. The same can be found with paper. One can purchase beaten

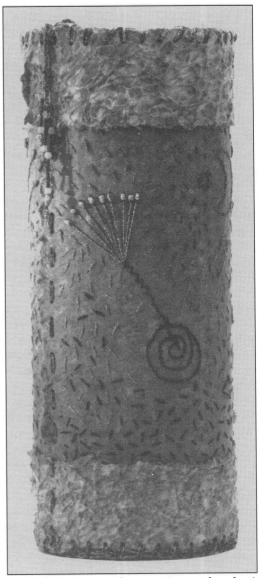

Bark Container, pulp spraying and embroidery, abaca, pearls, beads and metallic threads, 4.5" x 4.5" x 12", 1991.

Bark Container #3, pulp spraying and stitching, abaca, plastic, wood and metallic threads, 8" x 8" x 5", 1992.

pulp from paper supply houses made from abaca, cotton and flax. The following bark fibers can be purchased and then beaten at home: Japanese Kozo, Thai Kozo, China Kozo, Mitsumata, Japanese Gampi and Philippine Gampi. If you're industrious, your garden can be used to make your own paper. In the book, Papermaking for Basketry, in Sue Smith's section, she provides detailed information on using 32 different varieties of plant fibers, from sisal to yucca. Smith furnishes the reader with the plant's name, location, harvest information, how to collect, part to use, preparation and some interesting miscellaneous information on the plant.

As has been mentioned, 1 use a pulp sprayer to create my paper bark. Often the inner surface is sprayed with a darker shade of the colors that I am working with and the outer surface with a lighter shade. This provides some contrast to the piece while still remaining in the same color family. I have also blocked off areas of the top layer with a fabric and continued to spray additional colors. When the spraying is completed, the fabric is removed thus revealing yet another color.

My first bark vessel was inspired by Native American containers. While I was working on the piece a friend asked me if I were going to put my personal imagery on it. Those few words inspired me to begin embroidering with metallic threads and freshwater pearls. The smooth side of the paper, which is treated as the inner bark, is the side I embellish. The rough side of the paper, the outer bark, is placed at the top and bottom edges of the piece, similar to the old bark containers.

One does not need to use a pulp sprayer to create bark containers out of paper. Paper sheets can be pulled with a mold and couched directly onto a canvas or sheet. The side facing the sheet will be smoother. At least six layers need to be applied in order to have enough strength in the paper. Once a number of layers have been created, try experimenting with pouring some pulp onto the surface so the top layer is not so smooth. Designs can also be drawn in the paper while it is still wet.

An important step in creating a vessel out of handmade paper is to first make a template or model out of cardboard. Handmade paper is precious and it is heartbreaking to cut out a piece and then find it's not measured properly. Taking the time to create a model saves many precious hours of labor. Some vessels may need to have an internal form, which they are created over, that will remain inside the piece. This year I created an 18th century Dutch whaling ship for an exhibit in *The Kendall Whaling Museum.* The base of the ship was carved out of Styrofoam, for support, and this was covered with handmade paper. The old whaling ships were made out of planks of wood and that was how the piece was created. Each plank was stitched together and then images of whales were stitched onto the surface. The sails were made out of thinner paper which seemed to flow in the breeze. This was the first vessel I have ever created in which people did not ask what was supposed to go in it!

Past Lives, pulp spraing, embroidery and knotless netting, abaca, pearls, metallic threads and wood, 25" x 10" x 25", 1992.

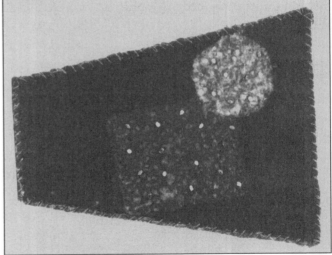

Bark Container #2, pulp spraying and stitching, abaca, beads, pearls and metallic threads, 10" x 5" x 12", 1991.

There are many techniques being utilized by other artists working in different mediums, such as bark or metal, that can be modified to work successfully in paper. Bark is often stitched together with leather, fine bark like elm bark, cordage, or waxed linen. Fine leather and waxed linen as well the many wonderful fibers on the market today, such as metallic or linen threads, can be incorporated into paper pieces. Some artists use different joinery techniques, such as rivets and plastic tubing, which can be modified to work with paper. I have found that, for the most part, the knowledge gained from studying how bark has been utilized has translated nicely into paper pieces.

Handmade paper is very versatile. The more one works with it and experiments, the more exciting and expanding one's art work can become. This has been especially true with my bark containers. The more I experiment, the more I learn about the fiber and its endless creative possibilities.

Shereen LaPlantz

Last year most of my baskets were twill samples (I was writing a twill book). Although I continued to make "real" baskets, I found myself loving the samples. -I do have a strong tendency towards sampling-

Consequently I'm continuing along the lines of the sampling.

Shape has always been my first love — baskets simply let my weavings have shape. Now all of a sudden I was weaving flat pieces of twill and folding them into containers/baskets! It was thrilling. With my love of research I immediately checked out bark baskets, folded geometric forms and Japanese gift box folding. The possibilities are endless — the only thing holding me back was the time necessary to weave the twills.

We know what happened — the twills gave way to solid pieces of paper. Then something unusual developed. I've always been interested in the outer surfaces of my baskets, adding surface curls or layers of open basketry and braids. Now all of a sudden the outer surface is less important. Books are growing inside each of my baskets! It makes sense. I spend most of my life writing, editing and publishing books. We have (literally) tons of books stashed around the house. Plus I read 2-3 books every week. They were bound to become an influence.

Every once in a while a new direction in my work becomes so compelling that everything else stops. Right now I have a year's supply of paper and my sampling table beckons. Slowing down to finish this book has been extremely difficult. We'll meet again when this "intensity" is over.

Twill Sample, 3-block twill, microwood, 9" x 9" x 6", 1992.

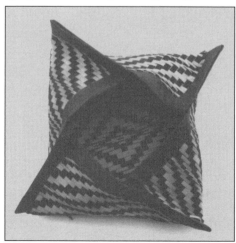

Twill Sample, diamond twill, folded form, microwood, 9" x 9" x 3.5", 1992.

Twill Sample, diamond twill , folded form, 9" x 9" x 3", 1992.

Untitled, folded form, unwoven book, paper, 11" x 11" x 9", 1993.

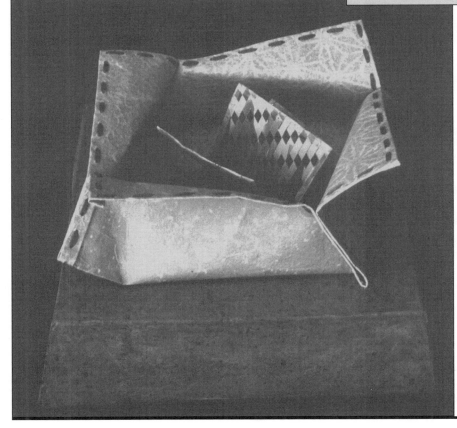

Untitled, folded form, twill woven book, paper, 13" x 13" x 8", 1993.

Carrie Nardecchia

Mary Summer Rain, In <u>Spirit Song</u> quoted an old Indian medicine woman, when she wrote "...in old days People love all stuff. They love trees, mountains, grass, animals, all stuff. Sacred powers were nature forces: wind, water, fire, lightning. Peoples know Father Sky and Mother Earth parents of all life. Every creature have spirit."

Each vessel is created for the spirit of a specific natural element. Nature, in its many forms, influences the shapes, colors, and titles for each piece. For example, *Forest Spirit Vessel* recreates the unique textured surfaces found throughout heavily wooded areas. The vessel's image is representational of my thoughts, feelings, and sensitivity toward nature's handiwork.

Constructed with handmade paper, the organic forms contain light free-flowing appendages which both adorn and protect the spirit's habitat. The vessels are created to entice gracious, generous, or helpful spirits within. As the spirits pass through the vessel's interior, they emit positive energies which remain after the spirit travels on. These energies are slowly transmitted to the vessel's owner and it's surrounding location.

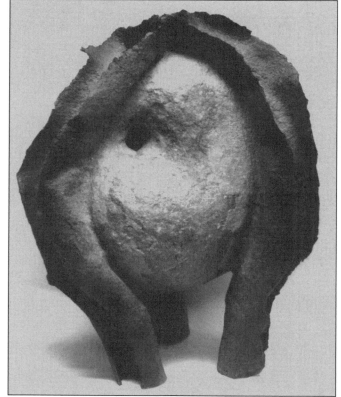

Birth Spirit Vessel, handmade cotton paper, 14" x 13" x 18", 1991.

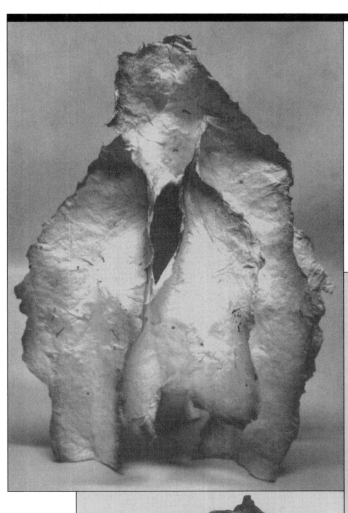

Bear Grass Spirit Vessel, handmade abaca paper, 7" x 7" , 9.75", 1991.

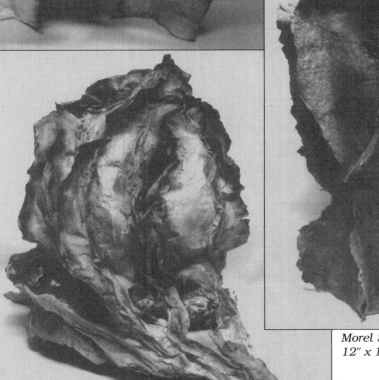

Morel Spirit Vessel, handmade cotton paper, 12" x 12" x 17", 1991.

Forest Spirit Vessel, Handmade kapok paper and drift wood, 11" x 23" x 13", 1991.

Helen Frost Way

The works shown here are a continuation of my exploration into fiber. Trained as a textile designer I was in love with fiber — and I eventually found myself doing sculpture. My work is usually a combination of fiber with mixed media.

I have been working in handmade paper since the later 1970's. "Offering Urns" is an example of blown paper over a woven frame. I pre-dye the fiber before it's blown or cast, then often paint or embellish it.

"Toro Xoreu," "Seeds" and "Warrior Maiden" are knotted linen thread. My interest in knotting developed out of necessity. An auto accident made it difficult to work in pulp. So I began to knot small studies for when I can again lift and bend as needed for working with pulp.

I have always believed in expanding one's knowledge of other media and techniques. Exploration of new areas creates new ways for an artist to grow. The most exciting work being done today is that which takes the traditional *craft* and uses it in a new way — a crossing over.

Offering Urns, paper blown over woven material, paper, material and dried lotus pods, each: 10" x 6.75" dia, 1992.

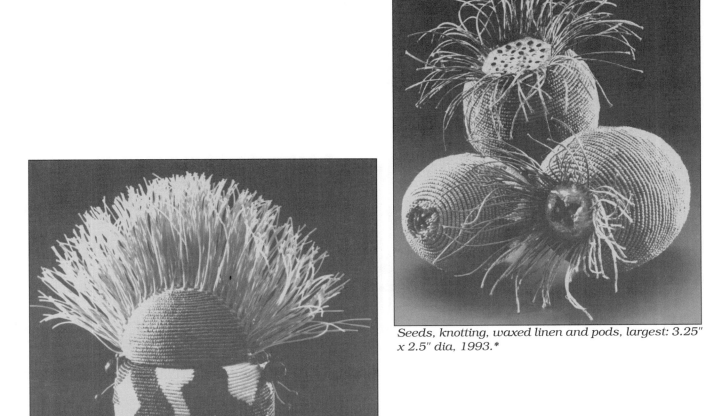

*Seeds, knotting, waxed linen and pods, largest: 3.25"
x 2.5" dia, 1993.*

*Warrior Maiden, knotting, waxed linen and beads, 6.5"
x 3" dia, 1993.*

*Photo credit: Rick Albert

*Toto Xoreu (Black Dance Skirt), knotting, waxed linen with
beads, 4.25" x 7" dia, 1992.*

Ann Richards

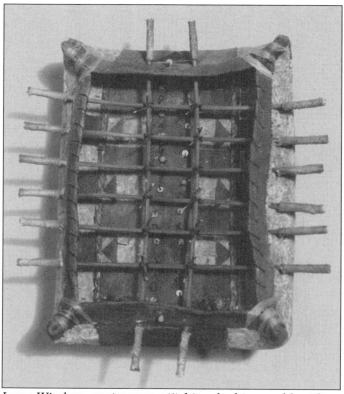

Inner Window, cast paper, stitching, lashing and braiding, paper, silk, raffia, beads, willow and waxed linen, 8.5" x 2.5" x 9.5", 1992.

Transcending, lashing and stretched gut, wood, rattan, gut and waxed linen, 13" x 9" x 10", 1992.

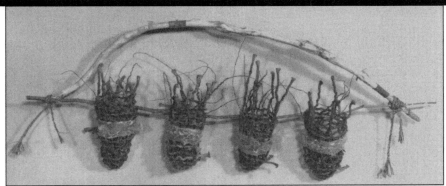

Family, plain weave, Japanese weave, braiding and stretched gut, inflorescences, gut, raffia, pine branch and willow, 17" x 5" x 10.5", 1992.

Familiarity with the materials enables me to create from within, instinctively. I try to limit myself to *basketry*, as the idea of a vessel form that can be defined in limitless ways, keeps me focused. It is sometimes much easier to create or to give an idea form with some limitations. I am confined to thinking in structural form.

During the creative process, I draw ideas of form that I feel best convey my message. I see my work as a translation of life, my everyday experiences reflected in my work. These are the experiences of spirituality, childbirth, grief and all human experience.

Concentrating on basketry has not proven to be limiting at all, but it has enabled me to push the boundaries of tradition. Learning from other basket artists' work and philosophies helps refine how I wish to express myself through my work. The whole world of basketry, *experimental basketry*, sculpture or the creation of vessel forms using traditional or non-traditional techniques is open to individual and personal definition.

Power Within, cast paper, stitching and twining, paper, silk, raffia, linen and bone beads, 8" x 8" x 9", 1992.

Rolled (recycled) Paper as Basketry Material

by Cathy Molholm

This technique of using rolled paper as a basketry material comes from Japan. It is both a simple and practical way to make unique and colorful baskets.

Although any thin paper can be used, one that is easy and abundant is the flyer ads that come with the newspapers. Papers that are thin, large, colorful and have a shiny finish are easiest to use. Some large sized magazines and catalogs also work well. Avoid paper printed with ink that will rub off on your hands.

Cut the paper to be used into long rectangles (ideal is about 8" by 20"). A small basket might take 50 pieces. Using a small size wood dowel, roll the pieces of paper in a diagonal direction from the bottom right corner to the top left.

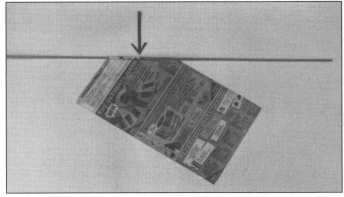

Roll the rectantangular piece of paper onto a dowel.

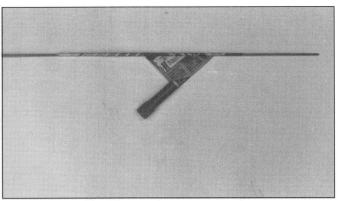

Glue the end with a Glue Stick.

Glue the top corner to make a tightly rolled tube. Because it is rolled diagonally, when the dowel is pulled out, the tube of paper made will be tapered — larger on the right and smaller on the left. The tubes are then joined together by inserting the thin ends into the larger ones continuously to be used as warp and/or weft for woven and twined baskets.

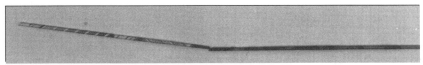

Inserting one tube into the other.

Below: Tribute to the Oaks, rib construction, rattan, reed and oak branches, 24" x 17" x 6", 1992.

Wall Street Journal, twined, paper, 8" x 9", 1992.

'53 McCalls Needlework Magazines, twined, paper, 10" x 14", 1992.

Group, twined, paper, 10" x 6", 8" x 9", 1992.

Veining in Twining

by Shereen LaPlantz

Twining is an incredibly fluid, organic technique. With twining it's easy to create undulating organic shapes rapidly. Unfortunately I don't see much happening in twining today. So -- I thought I would share one possibility with you. Amazingly complex line patterns can be developed simply by how you add in new elements. Let's take a look.

Twining uses two elements twisting around the stakes. The twist can either be overhand or underhand, it doesn't matter. But you must be consistent. Remember to keep your tension even.

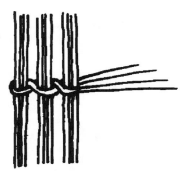

For line work I recommend using pairs of elements for the stakes. I also recommend starting with three pairs. Twine across them.

Now move the pairs until they radiate. Continue to twine around them. The second row of twining packs down tightly against the first row.

At this point I must admit that I've just broken my wrist and am having a terrible time drawing. So -- from here on please imagine lovely rows of twining. I'll only be able to show the stakes. (My illustrations of the twining rows look like black blobs.)

When the stakes are separated a bit too far, like at the dotted line, it's time to add in more elements. Remember, you're imagining twined rows here, think about three rows.

To add in new elements, take a long element and fold it in half. Slip the folded point in between the pair of elements. Do this for each pair.

If you continue to slip a folded element in between pairs of elements every time it's needed -- this incredible network is the result. This veining is quite lovely in a finished basket. Years ago when I primarily did twining I made many of these veined pieces as trays. Imagine how you can control the lines, how and where they branch, what type of drawing you can do with the stakes.

Susan Rowntree Boykin

Xanadu, random weave, reed, paint, wire, paper beads, sequins and waxed linen, 8.5" x 8.5" x 12", 1991

Photo credit: Jerry Anthony

Striped Quartet, random weave, reed, paint, waxed linen, paper beads and sequins, 7" x 7" x 9", 1992.

Lisa Grey

Neptune's Midnight Garden, coiled, overlaid and stitched, cording, fabric and paper, 18" x 21" dia, 1991.

Equinox, coiled, overlaid and sewn, cording, fabric, nylon netting, ribbob and a painted steel stand, 22" x 20" dia (w/ stand: 39"), 1992.

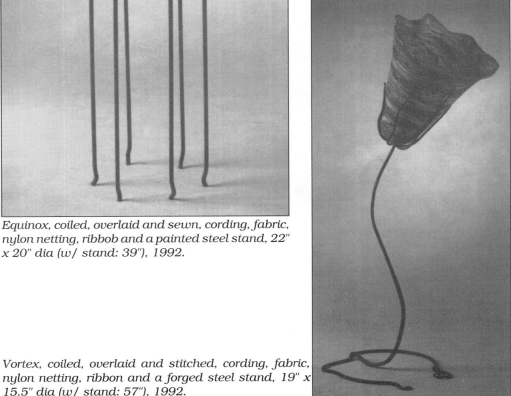

Photo credit: Dave Goodman

Vortex, coiled, overlaid and stitched, cording, fabric, nylon netting, ribbon and a forged steel stand, 19" x 15.5" dia (w/ stand: 57"), 1992.

The Twenty Year Basket

by Mickey Wilson

My introduction to this technique was in a workshop at Chastain Arts and Craft Center in Atlanta, GA where I was assistant to the director. I was interested in baskets, but not into basketry at the time. However, the process of single strand twining fascinated me. I started several baskets using a variety of materials but never finished a single basket. Over the years and as I became more knowledgeable in basketry this project kept surfacing. Finally I began another one and after trying a variety of materials, found yarn and fine/fine cane worked well to achieve the effect I had in mind.

Untitled, single strand twining, twining, chasing and wrapping, yarn, fine-fine cane, flat and round reed, 3.5" x 7.5" dia, 1992. Photo credit: Gordon Wilson

Bottom view

Another view

In order to use a single strand to twine, a horizontal inner rib is used to cast over and achieve the typical twine stroke on the outside of the basket. Yarn packs down nicely and gives a solid surface to the basket. The cane, on the other hand, gives a contrasting open work effect. Many variations can be produced by using different textures and colors of yarn. The selection of material is endless but the one necessary quality is flexibility. The stroke is almost like sewing and you use a large eyed tapestry needle with the yarn, but don't need it with the cane. According to the thickness of the yarn desired you can use double or quadruple strands. I used double strands of both the navy and white.

I tried several methods of joining new weavers. The most successful was looping the new length through the loop of the previous weaver, but you will still have a loose end or two to hide under the new weavers. Any way you can hide the ends works. It is difficult to work with a weaver over two yards long, three at the most, because it tangles easily.

I remember the instructor saying that this method of weaving was used by Muslims in India to weave their hats, using other materials, of course.

The rim of this basket came from a pamphlet from Hawaii on twining. There's a very hairy moment when you cut all the spokes flush with the top, but the twining is so tight that it holds and you quickly clamp the rim on and begin wrapping.

This basket taught me many things, but mostly patience — which I didn't have much of twenty years ago. It is an easy basket to relax with once you master the technique. It was a challenging project and a joy to make and has many possible variations.

S. Passle Hordinski

My baskets are hybrids from my basket coiling, twining, and knitting background. Due to unrelated hip and hand accidents I am unable to dance ballet or play guitar, but my vessels can whirl and perform for me. My silk yarn is knitted using a slip stitch to create a tubular knitting which holds the rushing. The tubular knitting acts like connective tissue, letting each piece move when suspended in a whirling, flying sense -or- curling, ready to slip into a new form. My twinning is also loosely handled so the rushing can have a life of its own.

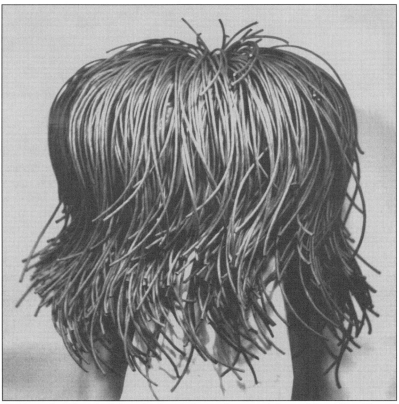

In Search Of..., twining (twined through a grate), rushing, 3' x 3' x 3', 1992.

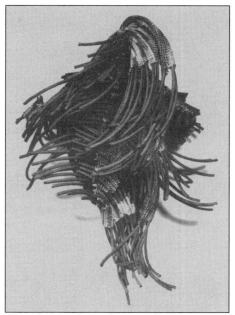

Whailing, tubular knitting, rushing and silk, 4.5' x 3' x 4.5', 1992.

Alien, tubular knitting, rushing and silk, 3.25' x 3' x 3.25', 1992.

Rushing, tubular knitting, rushing and silk, 4' x 3' x 4', 1992.

Jackie Abrams

My basket journey began in 1975, when I apprenticed to Ben Higgins, an 81 year old white ash basket artist (in Chesterfield, MA). For nine years, I made hundreds, perhaps thousands, of knitting, market and garden baskets. In 1984 I knew it was time for a change. I started experimenting with other techniques, forms, materials and colors.

In retrospect it has been a logical progression, influenced by many wonderful teachers. Some things have remained constant; strong lines, straightforward direct forms, with a basket technique or material always evident. The changes are more numerous; form, surface design, techniques, materials and textures have all been reconsidered. The most dramatic change is my use of color, starting with natural, muted tones and evolving to my current use of bold and vivid colors.

I am now exploring the extreme versatility of paint and paper. I can sponge, roll or brush the paint, selecting and creating my own color palette. Papers can be decorated, stripped, woven and stiffened. Ribbons, rhinestones or rivets can be added to the surface. The possibilities seem endless.

Double Ash Doors, random weave, notching and lashing, dogwood, waxed linen, ash, cattails and barks, 21" x 7" x 12", 1992.

Stamps and Ribbons, plaited, paint, paper and satin ribbon, 4.5" x 7.5" x 7.5", 1993.

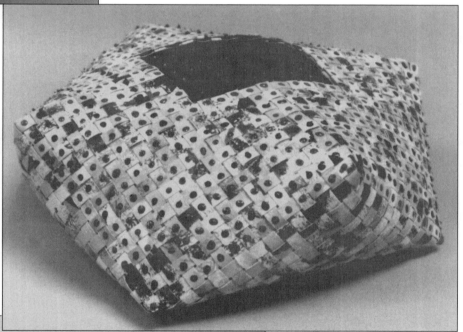

Red Dots, plaited, paper, paint, 4" x 9" x 9", 1992.

Black Sails, random weave, notching and lashing, dowels, paint, waxed linen, paper, ribbons and trim, 26" x 3" x 16", 1992.

Mayumi Tsukuda

Knot, twill, yew and Japanese cypress, 4" x 4" x 5.5", 1992.

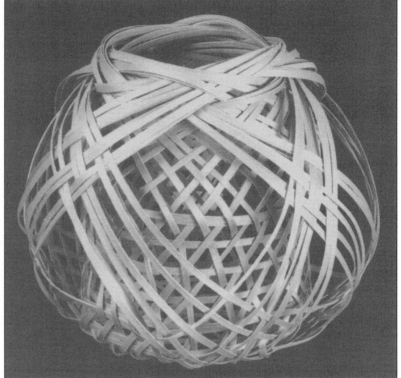

Flower Vase, Asano Ha pattern, black ash, 7" x 7" x 7", 1992.

Photo credit: Osamu Shoji

Split Face, woven, shredded money, 2.25" x 5.25" x 7.25", 1992.

Zoe Morrow

Side of Five, woven, shredded money, 2" x 5.25" x 6.5", 1992.

Photo credit: Charles H. Jenkins III

Five Leaves, woven, shredded money, 5" x 10" x 8.5", 1992.

Peg Personette

Stained Glass Windows, woven, dyed and natural reed, 9" x 9" x 8", 1992.

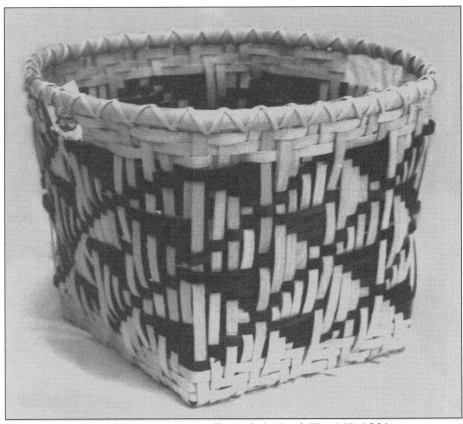

Samoan Inspiration, twill, reed, 8.5" x 8.5" x 11", 1991.

Coral Snake, twill with overlay, rattan, 4.5" x 16.5" dia, 1992.

Christine Lamb

Photo credit: Deborah Charnas

Sea Foam Twill, twill with overlay, rattan, 4" x 12" dia, 1992.

Joyce Schaum

The first few years of my basketry was spent perfecting traditional techniques and searching for my own personal style. Eventually, I found myself gravitating toward color, pattern, and classic shapes, with influences from Shaker baskets, Native American baskets, and Sosse Baker's twill work.

Many of my baskets are functional, but I truly enjoy producing more artistic pieces. My goals are to educate the public that basketry is indeed and art and a legitimate craft, bring enjoyment to others through my work, and not to accept anything but the best from myself.

Opposites, twill, rattan, each: 11" x 13" dia, 1992.

Cherokee Patterned Hamper, twill, rattan, 17" x 17" x 24", 1991.•

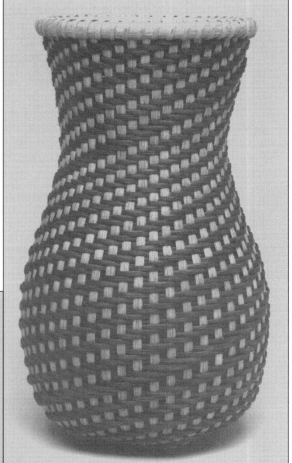

Twilled Vase, twill, rattan, 15" x 9" dia, 1992.*

Untitled, plain weave and twill, rattan, 13" x 15" dia, 1992.*

*Photo credit: David Egan
•Photo credit: Gary Schaum

Designing Twills By Quarters

by Shereen LaPlantz

Lately I've been writing lots about twills, but most of it is basic stuff. For a change, let's look into some complex design possibilities.

I look at ethnic baskets for most of my basketry information (my collection is my university). Many ethnic twill baskets seem impossibly complex — especially if the artists are working from memory instead of graph paper. So how do they do it? Apparently by designing one quarter of the pattern and then repeating that quarter.

This won't make sense through words. Let's look at a basket.

This is a rice basket from Kalimantan, Indonesia. Right now we're only seeing one side of it. The other sides and the base have different patterns! (See page 129.) Notice how complex the pattern is -and- that it's woven on the bias.

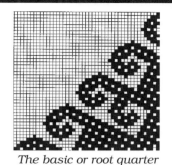

The basic or root quarter

Now let's look at the pattern. The key is that the pattern repeats itself based on quarters. It's also based on a simple 5 element border (these borders are common throughout southeast Asia, the Philippines and the Chitimacha tribe).*

*My new book <u>Twill Basketry</u> shows a 5 element border on page 109-fig 12, as well as several other borders.

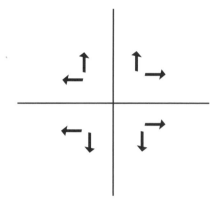

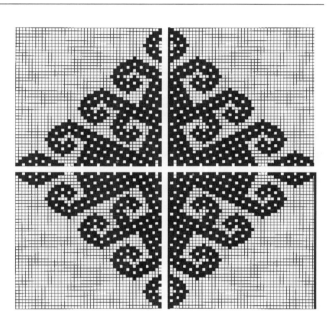

The basket's pattern uses the basic quarter *flipped*. Think of folding a piece of paper into quarters, that's the same type of flipping pattern.

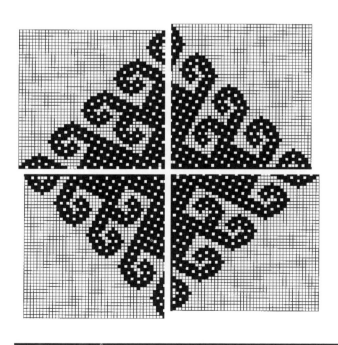

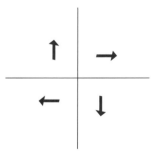

Now this is where the designing fun happens. The quarters don't have to be flipped. This pattern shows what happens if the quarters are rotated.

Before you grab the graph paper — you don't have to draw all of this out. Scan the quarter into your computer and let the machine do all the flipping and rotating for you. If you don't have a graphics oriented computer, use photocopies. Get the first quarter copied onto acetate — then you can do flips (flops, if graphics people are helping you), as well as rotates. Be sure to get lots of copies made so you can play with the pattern.

Turn the page to see what I mean by *play*.

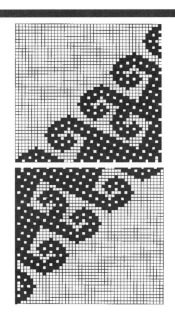

The quarters don't have to remain a full quarter of the pattern. The quarters can become simply a *component*.

Here the upper left and lower right quarters are placed above/below each other — making a line, a border. If you'll look on the next page you'll see that the border is actually more complex than it appears here.

Of course the next thing is to make the border into a pattern. Below it forms into a simple diamond. (Can you believe calling this simple!)

The problem with designing this way is — the baskets get big, really big. This diamond would require 180 elements across 180 elements. If you were using 1/4" wide flat reed, the finished basket would be 45" square! Perhaps it would make an interesting tabletop.

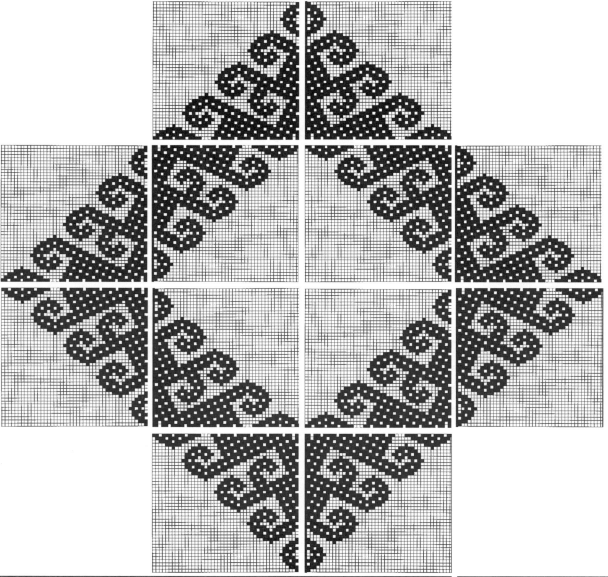

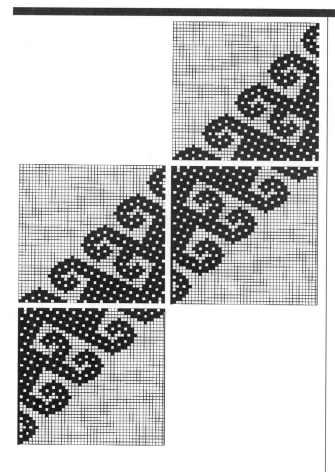

There are some other concerns when designing this way. There are a lot of empty spaces. These can't be left unwoven. They need some sort of fill pattern.*

The critical phrase when designing your own twills is *float length*. This refers to the distance an element weaves *over* -and- that *over* can be in either direction. When floats are too long they can get caught on things, snagged, pulled or just droop. Unfortunately there's no rule about what distance is too long. It varies — with material and with function. Something woven out of ribbon or cattails will snag easier than the same thing woven out of ash or oak. Therefore, if you're using a flexible material, the float length needs to be shorter than for a stiff material. Also, if the basket will be used in the garden or for shopping it has more opportunity to get snagged than if it just sits on a table. Personally I start getting nervous with a 1" float length -but- that's only my weaving background asserting itself. For most applications, I recommend being concerned with a 1.5" float length. If you have a 3" float, the basket better be made out of hardwood splints.

Below is another aspect of designing with quarters. This rectangle is achieved by not aligning the quarters perfectly. The rectangle may be exactly what you want -but- notice the little half circle at top and bottom. These circles don't connect to anything, and therefore become a problem. Cut them out — white them out. This type of designing requires adjustments. An area may need to be eliminated, a float may be too long, a connecting line too narrow, etc. Fix it. You're not required to keep the quarters virgin. The goal is to come up with a beautiful design, regardless of adjustments.

*Again, see my <u>Twill Basketry</u> book, page 111.

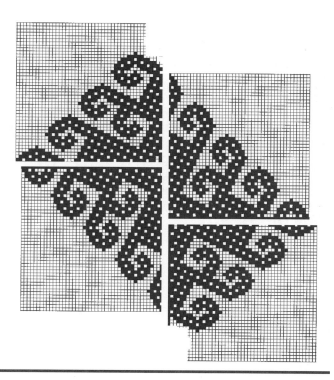

This is the full pattern from one side of the rice basket -- in a size you can see.

On the next page is the basic quarter used for this article, again in a size you can see.

For more information on twills, both weaving and designing them, I obviously recommend my book <u>Twill Basketry</u>. It's available from me -or- your local basketry supply store -or- the publisher: Altamont Press, 50 College St, Asheville, NC 28801.

One of the other sides of the rice basket and its base. Notice that the side is an open variation of the pattern in this article.

European Basketry Resources

by Joleen Gordon

Editor's Note: Last year Joleen Gordon conducted a research project on basketry resources throughout Europe. She has graciously agreed to share her information with us. This is not meant as an easy to read article, it is a resource tool. I highly recommend flaging this for futher reference -- when you travel. Plus some of the organizations have newsletters and/or books. Enjoy!

United Kingdom

The Welsh Folk Museum in St. Fagans, Cardiff CF5 6XB, is home for The Coracle Society. The society was formed in 1990 to bring together those people interested in the history and the making of these wonderful boats, membership £5 with a newsletter.

The book Chairseatlng by Elton Barratt, Johnson and Butcher has been translated in German for those who might be interested. Ray Johnson has written a new book on cane basketry, Basketmaking. It was released by Batsford in October 1992.

Sources of British basketry supplies:

John Excell, The Cane Workshop, The Gospel Hall, Wefitport, Langport, Somerset TA10 OBH. Telephone Isle Brewers (0460) 281636. Rush, cane, tools for cane and rush seating and basketmaking.

Dryads, Box 38, North Gates, Leicester, LE1 9BU A wide range of craft supplies including basketry.

Beth Hardcastle, 12 Charlton Village, Wantage, Oxfordshire, OX12 7HE. Beth's husband is making basketry tools, skeining knives and gauges for members of the British Basketmaker's Association.

Julien Torino, Great Braxted Pottery, Great Braxted, Witham, Essex CM8 3EF. Wooden rush tools, wedges and polishers and wooden willow cleaves

Information about the British Basketmaker's Association:

The British Basketmakers Association was formed in 1975 to promote better standards of design and technique in the practice and teaching of basketmaking, chair seating and allied crafts. One of their aims is to ensure the continuity of these skills by encouraging the production of tools and materials, and developing outlets for their work. They have an informative quarterly newsletter, day and residential courses throughout the year and annual bursary awards. They also have an index of experienced makers which is maintained to meet commercial inquiries.

In the past few years, they have made contact with The Worshipful Company of Basketmakers in London, the original Guild of London basketmakers. The Company supports the mandate of the Association with annual bursaries for its members and has given Honorary Membership in the Company to several of the traditional basketmakers in Britain.

1992 membership dues were £14 (International money orders in British pounds sterling are available from most banks). Send to: Hon. Membership Secretary is Mrs. Sally Goymer, 37 Mendip Road, Cheltenham, Glostershire GL52 5EB.

Information about The Guild of Straw Craftsmen:

The Guild was formed in 1989 to being together straw enthusiasts, promote the craft of straw-work, to raise the standard of straw-work and to disseminate information on all aspects of straw-work. Annual subscription is £6 for both members and friends. Friends receive the Guild news (twice yearly) and are entitled to vote at meetings, while Members receive these benefits plus their work has met certain standards set out by the organization.

Guild secretary Mrs. E.E. Carstairs, Conifer Cottage, Buck Brigg, Hanworth, Norfolk, England NR11 7HH.

The Corn Dolly Newsletter:

First produced in 1980 by the late Alex Coker and Janet Twigger to provide a link through which straw workers could exchange ideas and designs, advertise straw supplies and courses and submit articles of interest to other readers. It is now an international organization. Yearly subscription is £5 for 2 issues.

Secretary, Mrs. Janet Twigger, Crook Farm, 147 Hawkes Mill Lane, Allesley, Coventry, England CV5 9FP.

Information on American wheat weavers:

National Association of Wheat Weavers, Box 344, Route 1, Buhler, Kansas, USA 67522.

Information on Canadian wheat weavers:

Mrs. Sandy Kennedy, 1238, 2nd Street East, Prince Albert, Saskatchewan S6V 0H1

Heather Peill, R.R.# 5 Canning, Nova Scotia B0P lH0 is growing (and selling) several varieties of wheat for wheat weaving and would like to hear from those people interested in this craft.

Switzerland

My contact is Werner Turtschi, Im Dorfmattli, CH-3702 Hondrich, Telephone 033-54 7143.

Basketmaker Therese Leutwyler, Neufeldstrasse 6, CH-3604 Thun. Telephone 033-36 3268. She has a workshop and store.

Schweizerisches Frelichtmuseum in Ballenberg (The Swiss Open Air Museum), the only one of its kind in Switzerland. They have a resident willow basketmaker and grow willows on the site.

The Swiss Basketmaker's Association:

The IGK Schweiz (Interessengemeinschaft Korbflecterei Schweiz), Bernstrasse 9, 3117 Kiesen, Switzerland, telephone 031-781 2021, holds frequent exhibitions of baskets throughout the country. Their present director is Pepito Zwahlen.

The Freiamter Strohmuseum in Wohlen. Their present director is J. Rudolf Isler, Bunzstrasse 5, CH 5610 Wohlen. Telephone 57221518. A comprehensive book on straw plaiting has been published in German by the museum, Strohzeiten ISBN 3-85502-428-6. The museum also has a 7 minute color video showing the braiding and other kinds of straw work produced by the Swiss, available in French, German and English. Sfr 300.

The l'Ecole Nationale d'Osier Culture et de Vannerie de Fayl-Billot, the National School of Osier Culture and Basketmaking which was established in Fayl-Billot in 1905. The curriculum of the school is a 3 year program of apprenticeship. There is also a 9 month study period for beginners after they have passed a test to show their knowledge of basketry. They also have short-term studies for advanced basketmakers and for those who have apprenticed, but only after they have passed a test set by the school.

La Vannerie de Villaines, The Agricultural Cooperative of Basketwork, founded in 1849 in Villaines-Rochers, 37190 Azay-leRideau, telephone 47-43.33.03. The cooperative is not on a public transportation line so be prepared!

The Musee National des arts et traditions populaires, 6 rue du Mahatma Ghandi, Paris, 75116, is a treasure. This museum has an incredible collection of artifacts, including baskets, used by the everyday people of France. In 1984, the museum mounted an exhibition of their baskets, La vannerie. The exhibit was curated by Martine Jaoul who is the new director of the museum. The extended catalogue, La vannerie, was published in 1991, with 1000 black and white photographs of baskets. The price is 420 French francs, about $100.00 Cdn.

UNESCO headquarters are in Paris. UNESCO is interested in promoting crafts in the developing world. If you plan to travel to these areas and wish to help in a crafts related project, contact Mr. Indrasen Vencatachellum, Programme specialist (Crafts) UNESCO, 1, rue Miollis, 75015 Paris, France.

Germany

The Wannermacher Museum in Emsdetten. They have a beautiful video showing the process of making these winnowing fans, but the City of Emsdetten holds the copyright and they will not release copies. The winnowing fans originated in the grain-growing areas of Rome, Greece and Egypt. They were filled with the threshed grain and held by one man who gently moved the fan up and down so that the wind blew away the chaff leaving the heavier grain in the cup-shaped area of the fan. The fan makers did not regard themselves as basketmakers, although they employed basketry techniques. The fan makers of Emsdetten held the monopoly for weaving these large agricultural tools for the whole of northern Europe. One-third of their production was sold to Holland who in turn exported them to their colonies in North and South America and Indonesia.

Several people were involved in this industry and each played a role; often whole families were involved -- splitting the willow logs for the thin, wide stakes, weaving the bottoms, weaving the sides, and making the rims. With such a labor division, when one person goes, it is difficult for the others. Seldom does one person make the complete fan. They often formed cooperatives and helped one another out in times of social difficulty.

The Staatlichen Berufefachschule, the German Federal Basketry Trade School, is in the town of Lichtenfels, Bavaria. The school has a 3 year apprenticeship program, with no short-term study programs unfortunately.

Two basket museums in Germany: the Deutsche Korb Museum in Michelau and the Staatliches Museum in Kassel.

The week long festival of baskets, the Korbmarket, is held during the third week of September every year in Lichtenfels.

The whole town comes alive with baskets as they regard themselves as the centre of basketmaking for all Germany. They even have a street parade with a Queen; lots of music and beer!

Sources of German basket suppliers, materials and tools:

Andreas Schardt KG, Postfach 1224, 8626 Michelau, telephone 09571/8059

Hans Ender, D-8621 Hochstadt-Thelitz 12, Postfach 20 telephone 09574/1268.

Scandinavia - Denmark, Sweden, Norway

Denmark:

The Frilandmuseet in Copenhagen, the Danish open air folk museum has many baskets in the houses -- mostly coiled straw.

Sweden:

Craft classes in Sweden are organized by Saterglantan, Hemslojdens Gard, Fack 87, 790 30 Insjon, Sweden. There are two series of classes, those organized by Saturglantan itself (published in their magazine *Hemslojden)* and those organized by regional associations with instructors recognized by the parent organization. If you are planning to visit Sweden write ahead to inquire about the classes in the part of Sweden where you will be traveling. It is a very large country!

Karin Lundholm has written two books on Swedish basketry:
Naverslojd published by ICA bokforlag Vasteras (ISBN 91-534-0103-4) and Vasterbotten, Rotkorgar 4.83 (ISSN 0346-4938).

Norway:

The Norwegian Folk Museum in Oslo Has an incredible collection of buildings and artifacts plus a wonderful gift shop with crafts, including basketry, from all over the country.

The Viking Ship Museum has remnants of coiled birch root basketry.

The book Kurver by Jan Henrik Munksgaard is on traditional Norwegian basketry.

The Netherlands

My basketry contact in The Netherlands is Mia Pot-Van Regerten Altena, Gortersweg 14, 1871 CC Schoorl (near Alkmaar). Mrs. Pot is a founding member of the Dutch basketry group Wilg & Mand (Willow and Basket). She is very active in Dutch basketry research and in fostering international basketry connections.

Wilg & Mand was formed in 1981 to preserve the old techniques of basketry which were disappearing, to study willow agriculture, and to record the history of basketmaking in The Netherlands.

They have published three books preserving Dutch basketry traditions as practiced by Mr. A. Westendorp of Heerde: <u>Tenen manden, het vlechten teen ronde</u> (round-bottomed baskets). <u>Het vlechten van ovale manden met teen</u> (oval-bottomed baskets) <u>Geriefteen en andere bindmaterialen</u> (binding materials)

They publish a quarterly bulletin, Wilg & Mand (in Dutch).

They have a collection of baskets, now housed in the attic of the town hall of Eiselstein. They have a special donation fund whereby they gather money for special basket-related purposes, publication, purchases, etc for the society.

They have several special interest groups:

BOP is concerned with the description, condition and publication of research on baskets in Dutch museums. This is similar to the collating of information on the CHIN (Canadian Heritage Information Network) in Canadian museums.

Another group of members is finding out information about growing willows in Belgium and The Netherlands.

Another is collating information about the professional language, terminology, used by basketmakers.

While yet another group organizes classes throughout the country.

They have modeled their organization on that of the British Basketmaker's Association. At present, they have 500 members. Secretary: van Hemstralaan 35, 6814 KB Arnhem, The Netherlands. Membership 20 Dutch guilders, quarterly newsletter in Dutch.

Willemina Wendrich has recently written a handbook for archaeologists and ethnographers on recording basketry and cordage, <u>Who is afraid of basketry?</u> published by the University of Leiden.

The Tapijt museum in Genemuiden where they have preserved the tradition techniques of weaving rush matting.

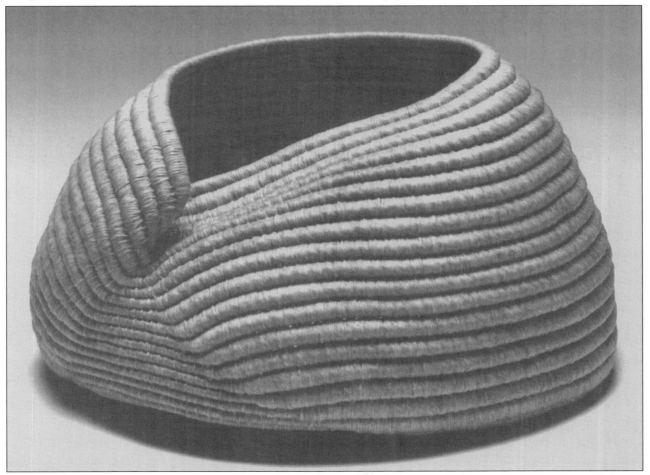

Sea Squirt IV, coiling, waxed and polished linen, 7.5" x 7.5" x 4", 1991. Photo credit: Julien Beveridge

Melissa Brown Bidermann

Wheel of Fortune, Fimo millefiori over gourd, Fimo and fourd, 13" x 8.5", 1991.

Blue Ribbon, Fimo millefiori over gourd, Fimo and gourd, 6" x 6.5", 1991.

Don Weeke

Petro Spiral, lashing, carving and painting, gourd, sticks and dye, 36" x 12" x 12", 1992.

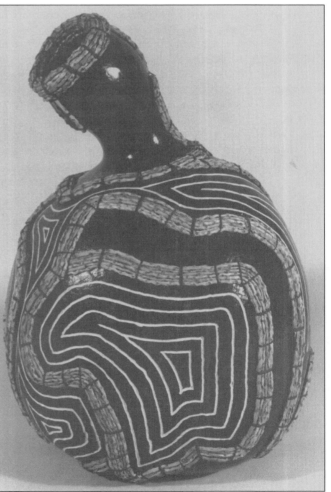

Linear Spout, carving and applique, gourd date palm inflorescences and paint, 18" x 13" x 13", 1993.

Gayna Uransky

Untitled, coiled, palm inflorescences and waxed linen, 10" x 7".

Untitled, coiled, palm inflorescences, waxed linen and driftwood, 24" x 13".

Suzette Nyokka

Untitled, coiled, queen and sugar palm inflorescences and seaweed, 20" x 28", 1992.
Photo credit: Martin Zeitman

Connie Loretz

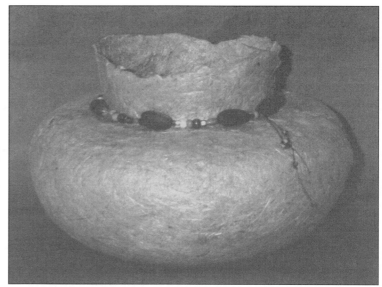

Iris #2, handmade paper, iris pulp, seeds and beads, 8" x 8" x 6", 1991.

Feather Circle, coiling, pine needles, raffia, cone and feathers, 15" x 15" x 10", 1992

Caroll Loomis

Faded Poppie Fruit Bowl, coiling, dune grass and raffia, 11" x 11" x 3", 1992.

Running Basket, coiling, pine needles and raffia, 8" x 8" x 2", 1992.

Star Flower Basket, coiling, raffia, pine needles and seed beads on leather, 6" x 6", 3", 1991.

Photo credit; Nancy Jane Ried

Kathleen
Peelen
Krebs

Canary Island Pine Needle Vessel (bottom view), coiling, pine needles and waxed linen, 12" x 12" x 5", 1992.

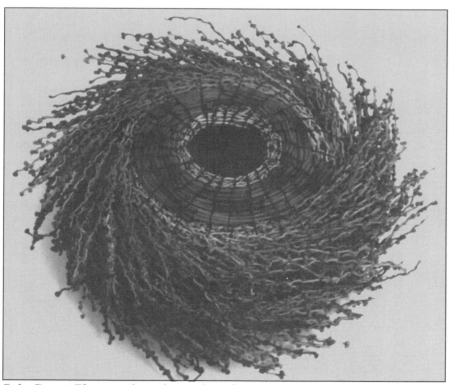

Palm Desert Bloom, coiling, date palm inflorescences, pine needles and waxed linen, 14" x 14" x 12", 1992.

Photo credit: G.F. Krebs

Untitled, coiling, pine needles, waxed linen and bone rondelles, 7.75" x 2.5", 1992.

Ethel Skeans Clifford

Untitled, coiling, pine needles, waxed linen and clay discs, 8.5" x 6", 1992.

Photo credit: David Klopfenstein

Basketmaking: Past and Present

by Joanna E. Schanz

BASKETMAKING: PAST AND PRESENT, a project sponsored in part by a grant from the Iowa Arts Council began with an idea presented to Iowa Basket Weavers Guild at their 1991 fall meeting by hostess Val Boyle. Boyle had researched Iowa Art Council Grants. The Amana Arts Guild agreed to become the sponsoring organization to apply for the grant since IBWG is not incorporated (it's very informal). An exhibit committee was formed.

Letters of intent asking for a commitment to exhibit were sent to Iowa Basket Weavers Guild members. Twenty-six members responded that they would exhibit. With a $10.00 per exhibitor fee, extra donations from guild members, donations from businesses and the $800.00 Iowa Arts Council Grant, *Basketmaking: Past and Present* became a reality. A notebook containing intent to exhibit sheets, gallery consignment contracts, inventory sheets, publicity information, bio blurbs, and artist statements was assembled. Black and white photos and color slides were taken.

Then the exhibit sites were confirmed: Des Moines Public Library, August 1-September15, 1992; Lake Arts Center, October 18- November 19, 1992; and the Amana Arts Guild, May 30-June 27, 1993.

Response to the two exhibits completed has been excellent and Amana Arts Guild is looking forward to showing Basketmaking: *Past and Present.* Iowa Basket Weavers Guild members come from a variety of

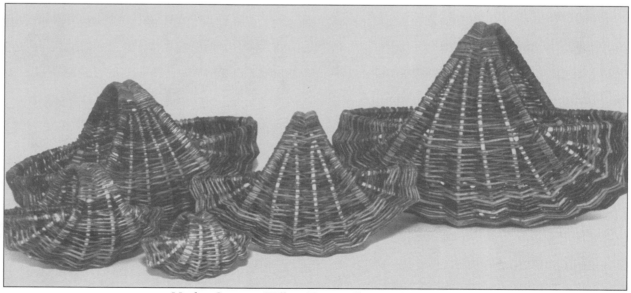

Marlys Sowers, Willow Nest, willow and dogwood.

beginnings with a variety of styles, materials, some traditional and some non-traditional. The few antiques exhibited show a connections between the past and present. About the only complaint so far is that we do not have enough antique baskets.

I would say that we have achieved our objective: "to propagate and promote the old tradition and culture of basketry; to inform the public about traditional and contemporary basketry skills; to make the public aware of the many artists working in basket; and to show the diversity of the art."

Footnote: As with all projects of this magnitude, mistakes happen. The wrong photo was printed in the catalog for "Mom's Sewing Basket" by Frances Struck of Bemidji, MN.

Kathy Kellenberger, My Bonnie Basket, cultured barked willow with peeled accents.

Laura Kleinmeyer, Lidded Sewing Basket, willow, barked and buff.

Joanna E. Schanz, Round Sewing with Lid, peeled and barked cultured willow.

Review photo credit: Joanna E. Schanz

Karen R. Thompson, Doll Cradle, wood and round reed.

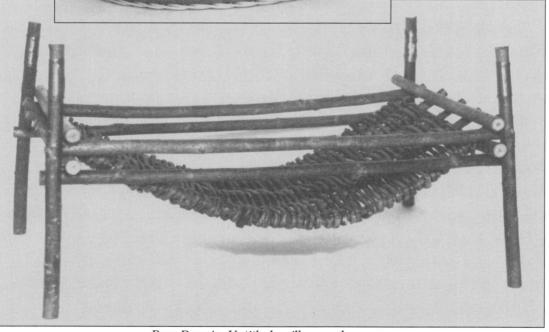

David E. Wortman, Antique Potluck Casserole, wood base and wicker.

Pam Dennis, Untitled, willow and copper.

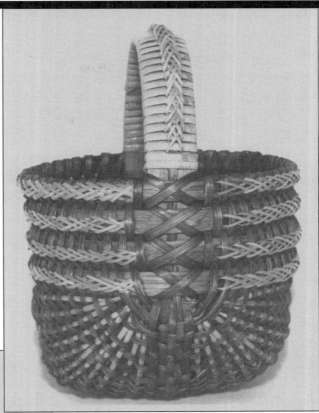

Margaret Wilkinson, Braided Cane, reed and cane.

Jo Ann Crane, Large Tote, dyed reed.

Jeanenne J. Craig, Jeremiah Basket, rattan.

Edythe J. Hill, Walnut Nantucket Style, walnut base and ribs, oak handle, and smoked reed.

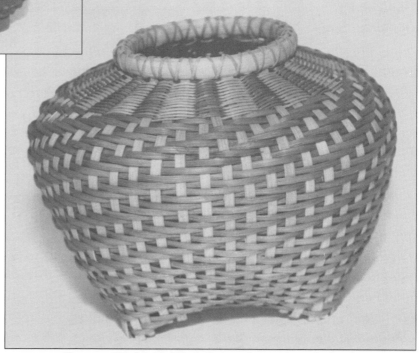

Frances Wight, Untitled, flat and round reed, dyed.

Pacific Northwest Contemporary Basketry Exhibit '91

by Mary Irvine

Basketry -- a part of a major Seattle Arts Festival? Yes! Northwest Basket Weavers -- Vi Phillips Basketry Guild was searching for a major basketry exhibition site. We submitted a proposal, which was accepted and funded, to present The Pacific Northwest Contemporary Basketry Exhibit '91 as a part of Bumbershoot, The Seattle Arts Festival. This invitational and juried basketry show featured the best in non-traditional and traditional basketry being done by northwest artists today. Focusing on the development of basketry as an art form, this exhibit opened eyes as to what is happening in basketry. Over 20,000 people viewed the exhibit during the eight days that the visual arts exhibits were open, with over half of those people touring the exhibit during the four days of the festival. An oft heard comment: "I'm never going to make jokes about basket weaving again!"

One of the most exciting parts of the exhibit was the range of work shown. Jurors Gloria Crouse, Jeanne Markley and Larry Metcalf selected quite a range of work. Traditional baskets included not only the work of Native American artists: Ed Carriere, Elaine Timentwa Emerson, Nettie Jackson, and Harvest Moon; and

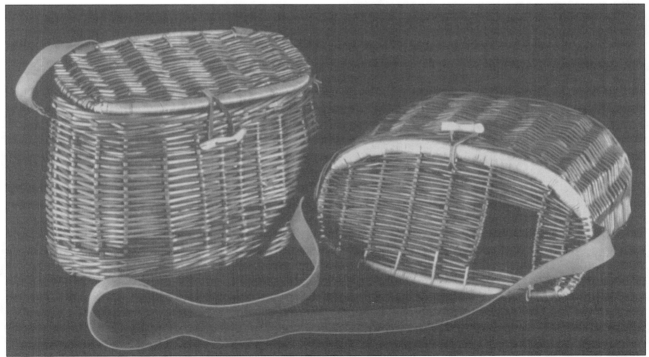

Joni Cashman, Pair of Creels, mold woven, German basket willow and leather, 13" x 6" x 9", 1991. Photo credit: Karo Thom-Edwards

Theresa Ohno, Lake Washington View, wrapped twining, cedar bark, bear grass and sweet grass, 4.5" x 4.5" x 4.5", 1991. Photo credit: Wilma Z. Ziegler

the work of those who have come to the Northwest to make their homes, the elegant Japanese baskets of Jiro Yonezawa and incredible utilitarian baskets of the Hmong, exemplified in the work of Nhia Hue. Not to be forgotten, traditional European willow work in the form of willow fishing creels by Joni Cashman, and Nantucket Lightship baskets by Vicki McGath.

Not all of the focus at the show was on the completed work. A display of natural materials gave visitors the opportunity to see the materials as collected, before becoming a basket. Throughout the exhibit Guild members demonstrated basketry techniques and answered questions.

Now, a year after the exhibit, the question is -- when is the next show? Soon! The Guild's proposal to present another exhibit, this time at Folklife was accepted and will be a part of the 1993 Northwest Folklife Festival, Memorial Day Weekend at the Seattle Center Coliseum. The theme: The Pacific Northwest Contemporary Basketry Exhibit '93 -- Celebrating Basketry in this the Year of the Craft.

Elaine Timentwa Emerson, Large Berry Picking Basket, coiled and fully imbricated, cedar root and bear grass, 13" x 9.5" x 15". Photo credit: Robert Simpson.

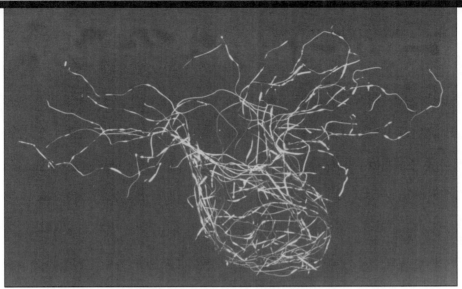

Manya Shapiro, Untitled, twined, stainless steel wire, 18" x 18" x 11", 1991.
Photo credit: Bill Bachhuber

Deborah Moskowitz, Wandering Willow, twined, weeping
willow, birch and madrona branches, 20" x 5" x 14", 1991.
Photo credit: John A. Gallagher

Mary Irvine, Cinnamon Skin, twined, gourd, rattan, gut and
oil pastels, 12" x 9.5" x 12", 1990. Photo credit: artist

Sharon Kita, Gonna Colorize? Add Moustaches Too!, plaited, film, mylar, metallic ribbon and colorized photos, 8" x 9" x 10", 1989. Photo credit: artist

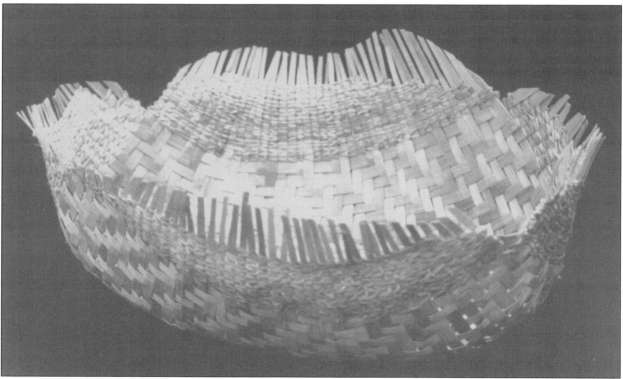

Lynn Isaacson, Earthworks: Lichen, plaited and twined, cedar bark, 12.5" x 7.5" x 17", 1991. Photo credit: artist

Crys Harse, Hot Point, twined and fold formed, dyed reed and oxidized copper, 7" x 5" x 5", 1991. Photo credit: artist

Donna Carlson, Untitled, woven, sterling and fine silver, .5" x .75" x .5", 1991. Photo credit and copyright: Randy L. Rasmussen

Dona Anderson, Plain Brown Wrapper, coiled, cotton cord and brown raffia, 18" x 18" x 10", 1991. Photo credit: Roger Schreiber

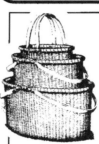

Index

Ethel Owen, Untitled, pyro-engraved an dyed, fourd and leather dyes, 20" x 8" dia, 1992.